T. FRANKLIN MILLER:

JOURNEY

AN AUTOBIOGRAPHY

Arthur Kelly, Publishing Coordinator and Editor

Cover and Layout by
Curtis D. Corzine and Virginia L. Wachenschwanz
Pen and ink drawings by Divid Liverett

Contents

Foreword

To have known and worked with a national church leader of the caliber of T. Franklin Miller has been a real privilege. Now to read and revel in his life story is a joy and special treat. This is not an autobiography written as historical chronology; rather, it is like a conversation wit T. Franklin—witty, intimate, full of amazing stories.

Franklin and I have been friends and colleagues for more than fifty-five years: across-the-street neighbors; partners in many projects for the church (e.g. international youth conventions, making the film *From Heaven to Earth,* creating the *Worship the Lord: Hymnal of the Church of God);* team-teachers of an exciting church school class. Franklin never seemed to engage in the ordinary, repetitious activities that fill so many lives; rather, he was forever being drawn into new, stretching, in-over-your-head kinds of experiences.

Here we find the essential T. Franklin Miller: his childhood poverty; his conversion and call to ministry; his courtship and marriage to Gertie; their talented kids and the family trips and vacations; his passion for his community. We are introduced to some of the remarkable people he has known as a world citizen. But we also glimpse simple vignettes: the joys of a being a rose gardener, the avid Rotarian, the meaning of the picture over their mantel titled "Jesus and the Children of the World."

Franklin is willing to share his own understanding of the doors opening before him, his profound insecurities as again and again he was called to serve and lead in new territory. He teaches us how life should be lived: pushing through new and formidable frontiers, being willing to risk, serving the Lord with all our gifts, maintaining an attitude of thanks for all. When we, his long-term friends, read this book, I believe we will join in a mighty chorus: Thank you, Franklin, for reminding us that the God-led journey is indeed our home.

Robert A. Nicholson
President emeritus, Anderson University
Colleague and friend along the journey
Spring 2003

Preface

Books, like rivers, sometimes have a single source, and sometimes the source is made up of many small streams each of which makes a contribution to the whole.

An early suggestion for this book came while the Committee on the Celebration of the Centennial of the Church of God was at work on its assignment. When the committee was making writing assignments, someone suggested that I should write some of my memories of my work as an evangelist and pastor as well as my work in the general church agencies. I chaired that committee, but did not give serious thought to the suggestions. In previous years the same idea was proposed during preparation of the motion picture *From Heaven to Earth.*

Recently some of my colleagues renewed the suggestion, so I began work on a manuscript. I am not a trained historian, theologian, or Bible scholar; those who are so gifted and trained I hold in high esteem. Some of my colleagues have given us excellent books in these and related fields and to them I will always be heavily indebted. I salute them; I admire them; I thank God for them and their insightful writings. What I give you here are chiefly some of my reflections and convictions.

For the last couple of years and more, I have spent many days in hospitals and health care centers without benefit of my books and records—and without my customary writing helps. That is an explanation but not a good reason for what inadequacies and inaccuracies are on these pages. A broken hip, broken again when healing was almost complete, plus other injuries from other accidents—all have slowed the writing process.

Acknowledgements

Nurses and other care givers have found ways for me to sit up in bed and write.

Our daughter, Sue Spaulding, and her daughter, Christy, have patiently typed my scribbled notes; my limited vocabulary leaves me without a way properly to show gratitude and warm appreciation for their invaluable help. My loving wife, Gertie, has been more patient, supportive, and helpful to me than I can say. Others in my family have given warm and frequent support in so many ways: Spencer Spaulding, Marc Boyer, Sandra and Tom Miller, Scott Miller, Gwen and Michael Spaulding-Barclay, Bill and Beverley Pitts, Dale and Dorothy Nye, John and Nancy Barclay—all have conspired to encourage, inspire, and give love and hope.

Several of my colleagues—Gene Newberry, Robert Nicholson, Carl Caldwell and others—have encouraged the writing. Neither these friends nor others should be charged with the evident errors or inadequacies for which only I am responsible.

Dr. Arthur Kelly and his associates Virginia Wachenschwanz and Curtis Corzine have given generously of their skills and experience in the writing and publishing business, and I am also in their unpayable debt.

It is my earnest prayer and hope that what I have written will be used by our Lord to bring hope and peace to some who might read these pages, and that due honor will abide with those of earlier days who have made the journey so delightful and joyous.

To God be thanks and glory.

Introduction

This manuscript is not a history in the usual meaning of that term. It is simply one person's reflections on much of a ninety-year pilgrimage of faith, with seventy or more of those years in ministry of the Church of God. I have called this "*The journey is our home.*"

I know many people who place great emphasis on background and heritage. I do not depreciate that; these pages will have much to say about background and heritage. I am grateful for my own heritage. I have great respect for historians and genealogists. My own brother was one. He dug up a vast amount of information about the Miller ancestors, much of it quite interesting. When my brother Howard was doing his family research, he found a disturbing bit of information. Somewhere in that line of noble and worthy Miller ancestors is also the name of a family member living on the early American frontier who was apprehended and publicly hanged as a horse thief. Howard's enthusiasm for genealogy fell to a new low. So did mine.

A friend of our family has ancestors who came to this country on the Mayflower. That is very important to our friend, who often inserts that fact into even casual conversation. I am more concerned about what is happening in our family, in the Church of God, and in our entire society now. The journey, not just antecedents—the journey is our home.

There are others who live constantly in anticipation of a future life, with rewards for the faithful and punishment for the unfaithful. I also believe in a future life and often reflect on it, but it is not a highly motivating factor in my daily living. "Pie in the sky" seems to be an escape from reality.

As we live, we are also writing history. These pages have a lot of history. As I reflect on the passing scene, though, I am more fully convinced that the journey itself is really our home.

In this manuscript we will look at a few signposts on my own journey of faith with a slight hope that it might be of some interest to others. We will look at and examine some of the incidents in my personal and family life as well as in our corporate experiences in the movement we know as the Church of God. Memory is one of God's choice gifts to us; let us cherish it. Memory can enrich the present and be beneficial in avoiding mistakes and blunders. I hope my story and reflections present our rich heritage and call attention to the flags and dangers.

T. Franklin Miller
Anderson, Indiana
Spring 2003

I

Missouri Beginnings

Dale Oldham's grandfather lived on a farm about ninety miles south of Kansas City, Missouri near the village of Horton, with Nevada as the county seat. My father was a tenant (actually a sharecropper) on that farm. The summer I was born, June 13, 1910, Grandpa Oldham decided to have a "brush arbor" meeting and

T. Franklin Miller's Grandparents,
Horton, Missouri

brought his own son William for a summer evangelistic effort. With him came his eight-year-old son, Dale, and J. T.

T. Franklin Miller's
Birthplace

Wilson. After four weeks of preaching, there was one convert—my mother. She was very religious, tenderhearted, and devout. Only as an adult did I learn that her own childhood days had been marred by her father's mistreatment. She cared for three small children—my sisters, Ocy Irene and Icy Maude, and myself. She attended the United Brethren Church a mile or so from where we lived.

My father was interested in the preaching of Oldham and Wilson, but apparently was too perverse to admit it. Unknown to my mother, he did subscribe to the Church of God periodical, *The Gospel Trumpet.* Each week when my father got it from the mailbox, he went to the barn to read it secretly; but he would not go to church.

My father had a rough boyhood. His mother died when he was eight years old; his father was an alcoholic, a sort of drifter who could not hold steady employment. His older sister became responsible for his care. He had very little education, about the fourth or fifth grade, but after his conversion developed good sense, intuitive good judgment, and a sterling character. He was converted when I was about five years old, and I remember him best for the days that followed.

From him I learned that labor is honorable and that a Christian is obligated to give his employer his best work. He taught me, by example, the meaning of integrity, dependability, generosity in all my relationships, and humility enough always to express, in word and deed, gratitude and appreciation for all who had helped me. From him I learned that a true Christian does not make excuses, blame others or circumstances, but severely disciplines himself to do what ought to be done when it should be done, no matter how difficult or unpleasant it may be. From him I learned to live on my income and not be bothered by the life-style of others, but to please God as a steward of all my resources. From him I learned that what is worth starting is worth completing, and what is worth doing is worth doing well. What a priceless heritage he left to his children!

Cedar Rapids Days

When I was three years old I persuaded my parents to move to Cedar Rapids, Iowa. For almost three years we lived in a small three-room house—that's three rooms and a path. My father got a job at the Rock Island Railroad shops and eventually became a drill press operator. We went to the Church of God, meeting in a storefront building, barren and dismal, with cold hard benches—nothing very inspiring to me or anyone else. But here I went to Sunday school. Against my inclinations and wishes, we

Sunday School, 1920, T. Franklin Miller', second from the right, front row

went to church every time there was a service of any kind. Before he became president of Gospel Trumpet Company, J. T. Wilson (the same one who came to Horton, Missouri) came to our little church in Cedar Rapids and preached one night. That night, after an intense personal struggle, my father had a remarkable life-changing conversion. He quit his swearing, smoking, and tobacco chewing; for the remainder of his life he was deeply committed to Christ and the church. I remember how, in later years, he lost his job. We lived on what passed then for public welfare. I remember many days of nothing to eat but cornbread and sorghum molasses. The bank fore-closed the mortgage on our house and we lost it, but I cannot remember the time my parents did not generously and at great sacri-fice give to the church every week. How rich is my heritage!

T. Franklin Miller, 5, and Howard, 4 months

My brother Howard was born in Cedar Rapids, Iowa. Between us there had been Emery, who died in infancy. In spite of a difference of four years in our ages, Howard and I became very close friends for life. Howard, I, and our sisters, Ocy and Icy, attended Harrison Elementary School. We played with most of the children in our neigh-borhood, which was limited in play facilities for children; it was a low-income neighborhood. Many of the

Third Grade, Harrison School, Cedar Rapids, Iowa:
T. Franklin Miller third from the right, front row

men worked where my father did, at the Rock Island Railroad shops or the huge Quaker Oats cereal plant. We walked everywhere, unless we rode the streetcar across the river to "town." (I'll refrain from men-tioning the long walks to school in driving rain or bitterly cold snowy weather.)

When I was eight years old I did door-to-door selling of garden seeds and, as an accomplished sales person, I sold "Art Velvet Scripture

Mottoes" for the Gospel Trumpet Company (now Warner Press). For a while I also sold original oil paintings by Ruthven Byrum, who was paying his way through the Herron Art Institute. His father, Noah Byrum, as treasurer of the Gospel Trumpet Company had enough "clout and connection" that he could arrange for Ruthven's paintings to be sold through Company channels. This was an early beginning of my connection with Warner Press, but I did not get seniority credit for those early selling days.

None of this made me wealthy, but I did learn to work. At age ten, I got my first real job, picking cherries for two cents a quart. One day I picked fifty-two quarts, earned one dollar and four cents, and promptly gave fifteen cents to the church—a practice I have followed all my life. I worked Saturdays and during the summer on truck farms. I planted cabbages, tomatoes, potatoes, and other vegetables; picked cherries, strawberries, gooseberries, and beans; dug potatoes, pulled turnips, and cut cabbages. How well I remember pulling turnips on bitterly cold, late October mornings, sitting in the cold barn at noon to eat a cold egg sandwich, a cold raw turnip, with cold water from the rusty cup that was kept hanging by the farm pump.

I also worked for three seasons for a wholesale florist, Art Bezdek; I did all sorts of work in that establishment. For most jobs, I was paid ten cents an hour, but one summer I worked on a farm that had produced a huge potato crop. The owner, Mr. Pierney, was able to hire men to pick up potatoes at fifteen cents an hour; at age fifteen, I was named his foreman at twenty-five cents an hour. That summer I made more money than my father did at his odd jobs. I seldom had a real vacation, but I always had a job, on weekends, during school vacations, and in the summers. I did janitor work, window washing, cleaned sidewalks in winter snows, mowed lawns, did various kinds of sales work, painted, washed dishes in a restaurant, dug ditches, and weeded gardens. I did anything honorable to earn some money.

At age ten, with Brother A. G. Ahrendt as my guiding pastor, I publicly committed my life to Christ. Although I had many unanswered questions, I determined to seek and do the will of God for the rest of my life—a resolve that never wavered. There was much in religion I did not understand. I was puzzled about baptism and a bit frightened, too. I did not know why or what it was except that all

I had seen of baptism left people wet, cold, and gasping for breath. A visiting minister finally explained enough to me that I agreed to let Pastor Ahrendt baptize me in the Cedar River. Pastor Ahrendt was the father of Kenneth, my best friend in those days and for many years following. Others who served as my pastor in the Cedar Rapids church included Lulu Malzon's father, T. T. Howard; Charles O. Lee; and later, Ralph and Ruth Coolidge.

Our congregation had many visiting preachers who usually stayed in our home and always ate some meals with us. Some memorable Church of God guests in our home included: F. G. Smith; H. M. Riggle, who brought his own coffeepot; E. E. Byrum; M. A. Monday; and Henry Clausen. John Batdorf came to promote Warner Memorial University in Eastland, Texas, and from Anderson College came both the women's and men's quartets.

Missionaries seemed to be either coming from or going to Cedar Rapids. I grew up with a strong interest in the missionary enterprise and wanted to become a missionary. The closest I ever came, I guess, was when Gertie and I served, in later years, as so-called "Spot Missionaries," first in Barbados, and later in Brazil, Kenya, and Tanzania. Also, both of us visited most of our major Church of God mission stations throughout the world, where I preached and Gertie sang. Both of us led conferences in many mission conventions. We became deeply indebted to scores of national leaders in more than fifty countries we visited on different occasions.

During my high school days, I had an increasing awareness that my life should be given to the preaching ministry; I was often encouraged in that by my pastor and by other leaders in our congregation. Unfortunately, there were no such things as guidance counselors to steer me into the right courses, neither in high school nor in later studies.

Two things must be mentioned about my high school days. I had great admiration and esteem for Mr. Owen who taught physics and chemistry; he was a deeply sensitive Christian. He led me gently into the world of science—a world to which I almost committed my vocational interest. A fellow student named Rudolph and I became intrigued with what Mr. Owen said about the theory of the formation of diamonds; they were probably formed when carbon was heated intensely and then cooled rapidly under terrific pressure.

Rudolph and I proposed an idea to Mr. Owen. Grant High School had been a school for the manual arts and still offered courses in mechanical drawing, pattern making, foundry, and machine shop, most of which I had taken. We proposed to make a pattern, followed by a mold, for a ten-inch iron ball. We would first suspend some almost-pure carbon (sugar) on a steel wire, then pour the melted, hot (3200° F) iron into the mold, throw the hot casting into a barrel of ice water, with resultant cooling pressure.

Mr. Owen immediately embraced and encouraged our idea and opened all the doors for us to get the experiment under way. In the shop, with Mr. Blakely's help, I made most of the things necessary—patterns and mold—and readied the cupola for melting the iron. Mr. Owen helped us get piano wire, almost pure sugar from the local Quaker Oats factory, and anything else we needed.

The big day came! Word had spread and curiosity seekers from the community showed up in force. Scientists came from the Quaker Oats Company, the Starch Works factory, and from nearby Coe College. Photographers for the *Cedar Rapids Gazette* appeared and a reporter from KWCR radio was there. We had everyone except Peter Arnett from CNN! We poured the hot iron, removed the red hot castings, and threw them into huge barrels of ice water. Later, in the machine shop, we cut them open. We did not find diamonds, but the newspaper gave us two full pages of stories, and Mr. Owen gave us each an A+ in chemistry and physics. Fifteen years later, industry leaders were making industrial synthetic diamonds using this very principle. It was great preparation for the preaching ministry, wasn't it? Quaker Oats Company offered to send Rudolph and me to college with a promise of later employment in their research department; just think how much better oatmeal would taste today if we had accepted.

Another memory from high school days did not have quite that exciting a beginning. I enrolled in a course in public speaking—a colossal mistake! I was so timid and fearful facing an audience that I literally shook all over when I stood up to talk. Today, I recognize that these were panic attacks. We had to give a speech every week; every week I would die a thousand deaths when I gave my talk, and every week I received an *F* for my grade. Miss Chapin requested an after-school conference. She suggested that I drop the course: I would never learn to speak in public, in her opinion, and the class was ruining my academic record that, until then, had consisted of straight *A's*. I said, "Miss Chapin, I have to take and pass this course, because I am going to become a preacher." When she recovered from her fainting spell, she agreed to give me one more chance. Friday—speech day— arrived and with it my previous fears, multiplied by a thousand. Fritz Baldwin sat in the second row from the front. Fritz was the school football hero; he had never once spoken to me. But when I stood there, frozen with fear, Fritz raised both hands, smiled, and cheered for me! Helen Rapaport sat in the back row, in the right, outside desk. I had often helped Helen with various math problems. When my whole body trembled and I could not even hold up my head, Helen gave a "stage whisper" heard all over the room: "Franklin, get your head up!" With that kind of cheering and support from my classmates, I struggled on to the end of my speech and was rewarded with a standing ovation. Even Miss Chapin applauded and later she was my coach for my valedictory speech at graduation.

After graduation, I faced the monumental question of how best to prepare for my calling. Our congregation was small, in more ways than one. It had a limited vision of Christian fellowship; it was unduly socially restrictive; and it generally distrusted education. Many of our pastors had worked patiently and diligently to try to liberate the narrow thinking of our congregation, but certain lay leaders, some my own relatives, were too ingrown and too arrogant ever to achieve "world citizenship." I knew I had to move away from this restrictive, closed atmosphere. I chose to enter Anderson College and prepare myself for the work to which God was calling me. First, though, I had to get some money.

I applied for work at the telephone office. With a great deal of persistence and effort (I checked on my application every single day for four weeks), I became a full time employee at Northwestern Bell Telephone Company. I did electrical work on the inside, where the cables and switching relays required so much attention. The company was preparing to change from manual phones to the dial system, a transition that called for a vast amount of technical work. Most of this was by contract with Western Electric Company, so I was given much-needed overtime work for inside cable installation. My work was satisfactory, and I was offered a full time job with Western Electric at wages almost two times the amount I had made at Northwestern Bell. It meant a career in which I had great interest; I was strongly tempted. I turned it down, though. Full scholarships had been offered at Coe College and Grinnell College, plus the career opportunity at Quaker Oats, but I followed my heart's and God's call and chose Anderson College, in Anderson, Indiana.

More on the Life of the Miller Family

My two sisters, older than I, had unusual names, Icy Maude and Ocy Irene. They were so different in many ways but we were always close to each other. Icy sang soprano and Ocy sang alto. Icy played the piano mostly by ear and often played for services in the Cedar Rapids, Iowa church. Ocy played a saxophone and for a few years was in our Cedar Rapids, Iowa church orchestra playing most Sunday evenings.

Both loved the Lord and had an unwavering loyalty to the church. Both quit high school before graduation and worked as telephone operators in the Cedar Rapids Exchange of the Northwestern Bell Telephone Company.

Icy married Leslie Sanders, a member of the Seventy-fourth Street Church of God in Chicago. They had a daughter, Janet; Leslie had a daughter by a previous marriage. Icy directed a volunteer church choir and became quite well known as a music leader in the greater Chicago circles of the Church of God. She died from a heart attack after many years of battle with sugar diabetes.

Ocy married Vernon Nye, a youth in the Cedar Rapids, Iowa Church of God. Ocy became a beautiful homemaker and devoted wife and mother. They had three children, Dale, Darlene, and Lois Marie. Dale is an ordained minister and was a pastor. He and his wife, Dorothy, live in Anderson, Indiana, and are very active in several roles in the Park Place Church of God. Vern served several churches in

Illinois and Missouri as pastor. Ocy was a very active teacher, leader of women's groups, and with Vern also a counselor and visitor. She died of a sudden heart attack after some years of illness. Vern then moved to Anderson to spend his last years with Dale and Dorothy. One of Dale's sisters, Darlene, lives in Cairo, Illinois, another Lois Marie, lives in Cape Girardeau, Missouri. Both are widows.

A brother of mine, Emery, died in infancy. I have no vivid memories of him.

Howard was four years younger than I was. We were not only brothers but very close friends all of our lives. He learned to play the slide trombone, played in the high school band, and sang bass in a quartet and men's glee club. He was a child in the years of the Great Depression. He suffered all his life from inadequate nutrition in those depression days. When I became a pastor in the greater Boston area, Howard moved in with me. He had attended Anderson College and later entered the ministry. During the New England days he became pastor of the new congregation Gertie and I had started in Rochester, New Hampshire, and then served in Bennington, Vermont as pastor.

Howard married Thelma Anderson, one of our own Boston young persons, before he went to Vermont. Later he and Thelma moved to Des Moines, Iowa, where he was pastor and did graduate studies at Drake University; still later they moved to Chester, Pennsylvania. He and Thelma had two daughters: Beverley (now Mrs. William Pitts) and Rebecca (Becky) (now Mrs. Pence). Becky and her two married daughters live in Indianapolis, Indiana. Beverly and Bill have two married sons: Dr. Richard, an Indianapolis attorney, and Dr. Kevin, a research scientist and professor at the University of Illinois. Dr. Beverley is provost at Ball State University in Muncie, Indiana. Her husband Bill, after a career with General Motors in personnel management, is now President and CEO of the Madison County United Way. Both are active in church and community life.

Howard was a coin collector and Thelma collected and refinished antique furniture. When Dr. Steele Smith was President of Warner Press, he persuaded Howard to come to Anderson and serve on his staff as credit manager and manager of order fulfillment and shipping. Howard was very active in civic affairs. He became the chair of the Citizens' Advisory Committee to the Anderson Postal Service. He became president of the Anderson Rotary Club and the East Side Community Club. Thelma died from meningitis and a few months later Howard died of a heart attack after a series of small strokes.

My father had only a few years in elementary school, but he became quite proficient in woodworking and working with machinery. He was treasurer of the Cedar Rapids Church of God for many years. He taught the junior boys Sunday school class and was dearly loved by his boys. I cannot remember many times when a repairman visited our house. If something needed repair, my father did it. He was a dedicated Christian who greatly enjoyed his religion—especially singing.

At his job in the Rock Island Railway shop my father kept a Bible and every noon following lunch he read his Bible. His fellow workers often made fun of him, yet at his funeral they came as a body and presented to our family the Bible he read carefully and daily; with it came their words of praise for his life as a Christian. It was a very moving tribute. He died from a heart attack following several years of suffering from diabetes.

After my father's death, my mother lived for short periods with each of her daughters, then lived for eighteen years with Gertie and me and our children. Many years before, Mother had a small sore in her right arm. All four of us children spent hours trying to persuade her to have it treated by a physician. She was firmly determined NOT to see a doctor. She was "trusting the Lord for healing." A few years later, when she came to live with Gertie and me, it had grown and was obviously a large cancer. Our family physician, Dr. Charles Armington, tried to get her consent for medical treatment. When she insisted she trusted the Lord for healing, Dr. Armington said he believed in divine healing more than she did. He had seen more. Mother knew he was a Catholic and could not comprehend his belief in divine healing. She persisted in refusing medical treatment. Months after that visit, she told me I could now take her to the hospital for she was ready to die.

I tried in vain to help her understand the doctors could really help her, and that she should go to the hospital expecting better health. Once she got there, the doctors decided her right arm should be amputated just above the elbow and we (Gertie, Howard, Thelma, and I) agreed it should be done.

Imagine mother's surprise hours later that she did not die but was quite alive. Months after the wound had healed she was learning to do many things with her left hand. She did some cooking, fed herself, did most of her personal care, and learned to cut patterns and use the sewing machine. With her strong interest in foreign missions, it was easy to take the next step and make clothing for the children of missionaries. She did this to perfection. She talked to the manager of our local J. C. Penney store and persuaded him to sell her remnants of cloth she could use in making dresses and gowns for girls. It was amazing. Then she fell in our backyard and broke her *left* arm. It was in a sling for some weeks. My dear wife Gertie had to provide constant care, including all the intimate details mother could not now handle. I know God gave Gertie unusual patience and skill in handling this new situation—she did it so well and with redemptive and caring love. Mother was totally helpless, dependent on Gertie for everything, and I do mean *everything*.

Life at our house often became difficult with personality problems, but Gertie remained sweet and lovely and both children experienced great patience and love. Mother lived out her last months in peace and simple but effective creativity. Dr. Armington came to our house one evening, sat with Gertie and me and conversed about life and death and the mystery of human suffering and the marvelous healing power of love. Mother was not aware and gently slipped away in peace. How rich I am and how grateful for this family heritage.

Gertie's family background was not the same as mine. Her father was born on the farm where he later lived, married, and had his children. He was a tall man with broad shoulders and thinning hair. He was soft-spoken and very gentle. He was a deeply committed Christian, tender hearted, scrupulously honest, fair, generous, loyal to the highest. He had the total respect of all that knew him. His wife came from a Pennsylvania Dutch family. She was an untiring partner with her husband, always giving of energies and time to her family, her church, and her friends. The farm was on the eastern shore of the Chesapeake Bay in Maryland. Mr. Andrew grew beans, some corn, tomatoes, and melons and marketed them locally. Gertie was almost in high school before electricity was brought to the farm. They had several dairy cows, many chickens, and a few horses. There was always very little cash money but plenty of nourishing food.

Mr. Andrew was a man of sterling character, beyond the slightest reproach. In his mature years he became totally bedfast with arthritis. Until her death his wife Minnie patiently and in great love cared for her husband while also managing the household and family. Both parents were exemplary Christians, loyal and faithful in all church affairs. Mr. Andrew gave the land on which the Federalsburg's First Church of God was built—the little brown church. For many years both parents taught adult Bible classes in Sunday school and urged all six of their children to be faithful in their support of the church. Albert and Minnie were close friends to nationally known Nora Hunter and her family. They were the attendants at the wedding of the Hunters.

Gertie was the only one of the six children who attended college. With the strong support of Adam Miller, when he moved to Federalsburg as pastor, Gertie made plans to attend Anderson College. The Adam Miller family made ways for the church to help Gertie with college expenses. For four summers she sang in a ladies' quartet, touring the country under the guidance of Rev. G. E. Sample, whose daughter Esther was also in the quartet. She came to Anderson College and while there she and I became good friends.

I was in Boston and Gertie was serving the church in Baltimore, where L. T. Flynt was pastor, as music and youth director. I tried to get to Baltimore more often then and courted that lovely woman as best I could. Esther Boyer Kirkpatrick, who was pastor in Washington DC, and a dear friend to Gertie, helped us. I would take the train to Baltimore, Gertie and I would go by bus to Washington, and Esther found many ways to encourage our romance. It was successful. One day Gertie said "yes" and we began plans for our wedding. It was August 9, 1938, in the Baltimore church, with Pastor Flynt officiating. Our honeymoon was in Washington and nearby Marbury, Maryland. The good people there were so gracious and kind, as were all in the congregation in Malden, Massachusetts, waiting to welcome their pastor's bride. It was a royal welcome.

Gertie was quickly adopted and loved by all in the Malden Church of God. No wonder! She is outgoing, friendly, cheerful, unselfish, kind, and generous. She is a gifted soprano soloist. In the years of our married life she has written curriculum materials for children and their teachers, is a successful Sunday school teacher, and often traveled with me to lead conferences in music and in teaching children.

Gertie Miller
Sunday School Teacher

She has been a faithful partner to me in our ministry, going beyond duty in managing the household (usually on a limited budget), loving and guiding Tom and Sue, caring for them and for me in times of serious illness. I have already mentioned her patience, tact, loving kindness, and skill in caring for my mother in difficult circumstances. She is a gracious hostess. Our guest books often have the names of three hundred or more persons a year being entertained in our home.

Gertie Martha Andrew Miller
Her Pilgrimage

I was born October 29, 1914, on a farm near Federalsburg, Maryland, the youngest of the six children of Albert and Minnie Andrew. My mother, Minnie P. Shick, was born in New Hope, New Jersey; she lived for a while in Lancaster, Pennsylvania, then came to Federalsburg, Maryland, when she was a young woman. She worked in the home of Rev. and Mrs. W. J. Henry, caring for their young children. Brother Henry had just started a small congregation of the Church of God, meeting just outside the town of Federalsburg.

My mother was young, beautiful, and a dedicated Christian woman. While she was attending this new and small church, she met Albert Andrew, a tall, handsome bachelor farmer. He was born on the farm where he now lived. This farm became the family farm on which later I was born and lived my childhood days. Albert wooed and won Minnie's heart, and they were married on September 17, 1888. My father donated the land where the new building of the Church of God was constructed, a building that stood for scores of years and was used for many church functions. My parents were the attendants for the wedding of Nora and Clarence Hunter, held in this same building. Nora Hunter later became the well-known founder and first president of the National Woman's Missionary Society.

I had three older brothers: Russell, Harold, and Virgil, and two sisters, Lettie and Florence. Possibly I was protected carefully and a bit spoiled by the older ones.

Russell, my oldest brother, always had a nickname for me which he frequently changed. One such nickname was Peleg, *which he had heard my father quote from the Bible (Gen 10:25) and I am sure he didn't know it was a man's name! Usually I didn't like the name he chose, but that didn't stop him. For a while he called me Lizzie, for one of my aunts.*

I remember that when I was about four-and-a-half years old, I became lost from my mother. She had taken me to town in the old Model T Ford car we had. Somehow I got away from her and walked down the street, crying and lost. A merchant found me and asked my name. When I told him I was Gertie Andrew, he knew my mother, and found her and took me to her. That was a very frightening experience for me.

Here's another experience I shall not forget. My mother had packed lunches for my brothers and sisters when they went to school. In each lunch she had placed a half of a banana, and then gave me a half of a banana for my morning snack at home. I knew where mother kept the bananas, so while she was busy doing the laundry, I climbed up to the pantry shelf and took the rest of the bananas, maybe four or five. I cut them into small pieces and went outside and sat by the garage door. I ate my fill, but had some left over, so I buried them. The next morning my Mother went to get the bananas, and there weren't any! She asked me if I knew anything about them; I was taught never to tell a lie, so I told her the whole truth! I don't remember getting any great punishment, except I was told never to do anything like that again without first asking permission. My humiliation was the only punishment I needed. I never forgot that experience even though I was very young when it happened.

My parents had a Christian home and we were taught what was right and wrong. Our house was a typical Maryland Eastern Shore country house. My father, who had eight sisters, had been born and reared in this same house.

After my parents married and the family grew, they added another bedroom to the house. There was a big kitchen, a dining room, and a living room downstairs. Also there was a large front porch and a large back porch. Upstairs there were five bedrooms; one was kept as a guestroom. I thought it was the most wonderful house in the world. We had no electricity, no running water, nor inside toilet, but it was my home! As a child I used to think I wanted to live there for the rest of my life and visualized the changes I would make in the house when I got older.

All of us children attended Friendship School. We walked two miles each way and it usually was fun. Everyday I looked forward to that walk.

My oldest brother, Russell, had already finished his seventh grade when I started in the first grade and it was a whole new set of children. Somehow I became almost a mother to the younger boys and girls. I felt very responsible for them. We stood together, and what strong bonds of friendship developed!

In bad weather, one of the parents, usually the daddy, took us to school in his buggy. On one such occasion we started walking because no one came to get us. It was snowing, and I got so cold I couldn't move from one set of tracks made by the buggy wheel so I could get out of the way if a wagon came. Finally, Mr. Fluharty, one of the fathers in our group, came to drive us the rest of the way to school. My brother, Virgil, just older than I, had to lift me out of the road into the buggy, I was so cold.

The schoolhouse was a two-room building and was heated by a pot-bellied stove that sat in the middle of the classroom. There was a stove for each room. We all huddled around that stove for a little while to get warm.

I liked all of my teachers, but Esther King was my favorite. She was my third grade teacher. She was gentle and kind; now I know she was a dedicated and committed Christian. Later she gave up her teaching career, got married, became a farmer's wife, and reared a family. One summer I was able to spend a week in her home and helped care for her children. I enjoyed that very much. I still get greetings and a letter from that teacher every year at Christmas time. As I write this, she is ninety years old. While I was in grade school, I often brought friends home to spend the night with me. My parents were always glad to have them as visitors.

I left Friendship School after the sixth grade and began attending the school in town. I was homesick for my former classmates, but I was a good student and was conscientious about my work.

There was not very much money available in our home, so I had to work and earn money to buy practically all of my clothes. In the spring I picked strawberries. In the summer I worked in the tomato factory, and my father would pay us a little bit to pick cucumbers, tomatoes, and other vegetables on the home farm. I worked in the fields a great deal, but never drove a team of horses for plowing or for cultivating.

My main chore at home was keeping the wood box filled with firewood for cooking on the kitchen range and for heating the other stove used to heat the rest of the house. We all slept in unheated bedrooms, often taking a hot iron wrapped in flannel cloth to bed with us to keep our feet warm.

I was very active in high school. I sang in the glee club, played on the girl's athletic teams, was captain of the volleyball team, playing center position. I had a wonderful time and always stayed on the honor roll.

I was permitted to attend the Junior-Senior Prom because there would not be any dancing; we were all dressed in our best clothes, though, and we had a lot of fun. It didn't matter whether or not one had a date.

In my senior year I had the lead role in the senior class play and was second highest scholastically in my class. This permitted me to make one of the speeches at my graduation.

Just prior to graduation, perhaps a year or so before, Dr. Adam Miller and his wife, Grace, came from Japan with their family to become our pastors. Before that time we did not have a youth group in our church and there was not much incentive for us young people to go to church except for Sunday school. Now the Millers organized a youth group and it was wonderful. It drew many young people from the community. I never missed a meeting.

I was beginning to realize that I needed to make a commitment to Christ. The pressure of my peers was very strong, and I faced many temptations to do things I knew would not be right. At a youth convention held in Baltimore, Maryland, I gave my life to Christ in a full and unreserved commitment at an altar of prayer. I never turned back or regretted that decision. It became a pivotal point in my life. Pastor Miller and his wife gave me a lot of responsibility, mostly in youth work, but I also became very active in many other aspects of the work of our congregation of the Church of God.

I really wanted to go to college and prepare to become a teacher, but it appeared there was no way that could be done. My parents couldn't send me, so what was I to do? The Millers wanted me to attend Anderson College and would just not let me say, "No!" So they asked members of the congregation for pledges to help pay my college expenses. Today the amount they pledged seems very small, but at that time and for those people it was a lot of money. Some families pledged a dollar a week, and others seventy-five cents or fifty cents a week. All of the pledges together made enough to pay my tuition for the first year.

After I got to Anderson and was a full-time college student, I worked wherever I could to raise the rest of the money needed, and from that time on I was on my own. There were many times when I did not know how I would get money to pay the expenses, but the Lord was watching over me and always opened a door when to me it appeared to be closed.

About this time my father's health began to fail. He was seventy-one years old and had never had a serious illness in his life. He was a hard worker and had lived a clean life. Now the doctor diagnosed the illness as crippling arthritis. In those days and in that place not much could be done to cure such an illness. In six months he was no longer able to walk at all. Since he had never been sick, he had a low threshold for pain.

He did not easily cope with this disaster, nor did the rest of us. It was a shock to all of us. I was home for the summer months, and I felt guilty in planning to leave home for another year in college.

I sought help and counsel and was advised that there was nothing I could do to help if I stayed home, so I returned to Anderson College. I guess that has haunted me all these years.

My father lived fourteen years longer, but was totally helpless, completely dependent on members of the family for all of his care. In spite of his pain and distress, he was always alert, with a healthy mental attitude, and he remained dedicated to the Lord. He kept a radiant faith and was a living witness to all who came to call on him. His illness was very hard on my mother, on my brother, Virgil, and my sister, Florence, who were still living at home.

During my second year at college, I became a member of a ladies quartet. On weekends and through the summer months, we traveled extensively, singing in churches all across the United States. It was not always easy, but we met hundreds of wonderful people, and to this day I still meet those who remember when I stayed in their home or sang in their church. Enough money came in from the offerings for my tuition, food, and lodging. I was able to finish four years and graduated with a bachelor of arts degree.

On one of our trips in the summer, we visited my home church to give a Sunday morning concert. My family had arranged to get my father into a car and they brought him to church. Our quartet was already in the chancel area, ready to sing when the doors opened and two friends carried in my father and gently placed him in a pew. It was a very emotional time for me, as indeed it was for everyone in the building. My father was greatly loved by all who knew him. In spite of his crippling illness, he maintained his optimism, radiance, joy, and faith in God and his love for his family and friends.

Just before I left the Anderson College campus after graduation, I had my first date with Franklin. He soon let me know he was serious, but he (so to speak) had first to break up another romance of mine. I was not ready for anything like this; I couldn't shift gears that fast. I went to Baltimore, where I became choir director and director of Christian education for the First Church of God. The Pastor was L. T. Flynt. I loved my work and soon made new friends, some of whom are still close friends to this day.

Franklin was a pastor in greater Boston and I was in Baltimore; he was insistent, and our romance blossomed. One year later we were married in the Baltimore Church of God, and I went to Everett, Massachusetts, as a new bride and a pastor's wife. I loved Franklin and I loved the pastoral ministry. I gave myself fully to it as Franklin's helpmate. I became deeply involved in the lives of those in our church and many others that became friends. Franklin and I wanted to start a family, even though we were poorer than anyone can imagine—and I DO MEAN POOR! He was being paid fifteen dollars a week. Even if you apply inflation, that really wasn't much of a salary. We wanted a baby anyway and were disappointed when my first pregnancy ended in a miscarriage.

Later, some three years after we were married, our first child, Tommy, was born. He filled our lives with joy and I had another one to live for. What a beautiful child he was. He was deeply loved by everyone in our church. We were very happy in our work, but Franklin was called to a new position in Anderson, Indiana, and with many tears and great reluctance, we went.

We moved to Anderson, Indiana when Tommy was three years old. Franklin was named secretary of home missions for the Board of Church Extension and Home Missions. The board owned a house on Ruddle Avenue in Anderson. We were able to rent it from them, and later applied the rental payments to its purchase.

The Pastor and Family at Everett

Our second child was born in May 1944, a beautiful little blue-eyed dark-haired daughter we named Joan Esther. The baby was stillborn, and

Franklin was advised by the hospital authorities to arrange at once for a funeral director to come, so I did not get to see my baby. She was buried in Maplewood Cemetery. Our lives were shattered. I grieved for a long time, until I knew I was pregnant again. In August 1945, our beautiful blonde, blue-eyed daughter Sue Ellen was born, and how we rejoiced and thanked the Lord.

I was feeling the weight of responsibility very keenly now. Franklin had to travel a lot and I had the two children to care for; I felt very inadequate for everything. I suffered an emotional breakdown. I remember several foggy months of trying to find my way through this depression. Franklin supported me all the way; also Dean Russell Olt was a great help to me and to Franklin. When I was able to carry my responsibilities again, I still took my work very seriously and tried to give my very best.

When Sue was two years old, Franklin's mother came to live with us. She had a large ugly cancer on her right arm, just below the elbow. She refused to have it removed. She was "waiting for God to heal her." It grew much worse, and she became bedfast. I had to care for her. Her room was upstairs and many times every day I ran up and down those stairs. I had no other help in the home, and with two young children to care for, it was wearing me down. Franklin told his Mother she would have to get medical care and gradually she began to understand this.

Dr. Charles Armington, our family physician, a kind, loving, capable Christian doctor, came to see her, and placed her in the hospital, largely against her wishes. She finally consented to have surgery, and they amputated her right arm just below the elbow. For her this was very traumatic, but eventually she adjusted. In a few months the arm healed and she began to find a new purpose in life. She learned to sew, using her left hand. She made clothes for children of missionaries and outfitted several missionary families.

T. Franklin Miller's mother, Mabel, with hand sewn clothes

She lived for another eighteen years and made her home with us. (If Franklin were writing this, he probably would say something about the difficulties of those years. While his mother learned to do many things, she still required a lot of assistance with many personal matters. I helped wash her hair and cared for it. He would also mention that once she broke her left arm, and for a long time she was totally dependent for all the intimate matters of personal care. He would also mention that she was not at all easy to live with, for me or for him, or for the children. He would also say that the Lord helped us daily and we managed to get through.)

As the children grew, along with my role as wife and mother, I became more active in the church and community affairs. I often sang solos, sang in the choir, wrote curriculum lessons for the national work of Sunday school, taught Sunday school, served as a den mother and as a leader for Brownie Scouts, and Cub Scouts.

I never felt that my life wasn't full as a homemaker and support to Franklin. I found real joy in opening our home to many missionaries and national church workers. We tried to expose our children to the very cream of leaders of the Church of God worldwide and to leaders of many other religious groups. Our many guest books are filled with names of persons from all over the United States and from countries all around the world. Life was rich and full.

When Franklin left the Board of Church Extension and Home Missions after two years of hectic service and not always pleasant employment, he became the executive secretary of the national Board of Christian Education. Dr. A. T. Rowe, who was president of what is now Warner Press (then Gospel Trumpet Company) encouraged us to find a suitable lot and build our own house. With his help we got three lots on what is now 1210 East Seventh Street. Russell Byrum agreed to be the builder and was very kind and generous in getting this house built. Those were difficult years for us in many ways, not least of which was financial. (Franklin often said we built this house on a shoestring—one that was broken and tied several times!) We tried to be good stewards of all our resources, and handled our money very carefully. We are so glad, for we have enjoyed this house and its grounds so much through these years; it really became home to our family.

The Lord gave me strength and guidance through all those years. I often sang solos in the Park Place Church of God. I well remember the first time Tom accompanied me on the piano in the Park Place Church. He was about twelve-years-old, and I think maybe he was as thrilled as I was.

Those were busy years, watching the children grow through childhood to teenagers and on to college. They were good years. We tried so hard to build solidarity into our family life. We worked hard at creating togetherness, sometimes helped and sometimes hindered by the extensive travel and many appointments Franklin had with his work. When we could do so, especially in the summer months, we traveled as a family for some of Franklin's many appointments and engagements across the United States. Once in a while we were able to combine a brief winter or Easter vacation period with some of those travels. It took a lot of planning, but we thought it was worth it, and we hope our children did also.

Tom began studying piano with Charlotte Brooks at a very early age. He studied with others as he got older, including Dr. Paul Breitweiser. By the time he was in college he was an excellent musician with special skills in piano music. One thing that worried us very much in his high school years was his intense love for jazz. Not only did he like it, he performed extremely well, and it worried us. He would sit at the piano and play jazz music over and over. We didn't want to discourage him from taking piano lessons, so we tried to be patient and to say little. We really thought that with the heavy beat of his foot he might wear a hole in the rug! We wondered what we had done wrong and were concerned that he might join a jazz band; in fact, he was offered just that very option, but he did not accept it. Well, anyway, somewhere down the road he made a "right" turn and followed a career in church choral music. He still likes jazz, and Franklin and I finally learned that what Tom says is real jazz isn't so bad, after all!

Sue was also a gifted musician. On the piano Tom played strictly by the notes; Sue was also an excellent reader, but she could play practically anything she heard, with or without notes. She also studied under Dr. Breitweiser and others. She was especially gifted in improvisation. She could play for an hour at a time, without a book to follow, and never repeat a song, and did it well. She accompanied me often. Then she began taking organ lessons under Shirley Coolidge and developed skill as an organist. She served various churches as organist, and on occasion played the organ at Park Place Church of God. We have thanked God so often that Tom and Sue had such native gifts in music, developed those talents, and have kept them dedicated to the glory of God.

How we enjoyed the young people Tom and Sue brought into our home through the years—classmates, friends, and neighbors. How we enjoyed sharing our table with their friends and with ours. The guest books we have kept for over fifty years have the signatures of people it has been our pleasure to entertain; we enjoy looking through those books and living again in memory some of those delightful experiences.

We watched (sometimes with concern) as Tom and then Sue had their romances, and rejoiced in their choices of life-mates. Tom was married to a beautiful and gifted young lady, Sandra Haynes, from Wichita, Kansas, an Anderson College graduate. He left our nest. Four years later Sue was married to a handsome and talented Anderson College graduate, Spencer Spaulding, from Brookings, South Dakota. Now both children were gone, and we were back where we started, just the two of us.

At first we felt the terrible emptiness, but gradually I learned that now I could travel with Franklin, and more and more I could do some of those things I had always wanted to do. I volunteered for work at Community Hospital and did this for ten years. I directed a choir for retirees at our church for five years. More and more I worked in the garden with flowers and vegetables. We did some extensive travel in other countries, including a ten-week trip around the world. We volunteered for short-term missionary service, first in Barbados and then in Brazil. Those were challenging, growing, and delightful experiences.

We thought we would never become grandparents. After Tom was married, he and Sandra went on to get Masters Degrees in music, he in choral and she in organ. Then Tom went on to get his Doctor's Degree in Music Education, They delayed having a child until that was accomplished.

Then, after eight years of their marriage, our wonderful grandson Scott was born. We welcomed him into our hearts and lives. Likewise, Sue and Spencer continued their education, Spencer with a master of divinity degree, and waited five years before their first child Gwen was born. She was a beautiful blue-eyed blonde. Spencer at this time was pastor of a congregation of the Church of God. Three years after the birth of Gwen, Christy came into the Spaulding family, another beautiful baby with dark hair. Life took on new meaning with the coming of our grandchildren. We adored them and visited them or arranged for them to visit use very time we could—how rich life is!

Tom and Sandy moved to Portland, Oregon, where Tom became director of choral music for Warner Pacific College. Sue and Spencer were in Scotland for three years while Spencer did graduate studies at the University of St. Andrews. Twice we visited the Spaulding family while they were in Scotland. We tried so hard to keep in touch with our children and their families.

When Sue and Spencer and their daughters left Scotland, they moved to Anderson, and Spencer and Sue began teaching at Anderson College. We have been privileged to be close to Gwen and Christy so we could watch them grow. We tried to visit Tom and Sandy about twice a year, and for many summers they would put Scott on the plane and he would fly to Indiana to spend a couple of weeks with us. We became very close to him, also. We have watched each of these wonderful persons make crucial decisions and mature as they assumed more responsibility. We surely are proud of Scott, Gwen, and Christy.

Now, as I write this, Scott is studying in Frieburg, Germany for this year. He will return and will graduate from Linfield College, in Oregon, in the spring. He will be twenty-two-years old in June! Gwen will be twenty-one in March, and is a junior at Anderson University. Christy, soon to be eighteen, is a senior at Highland High School. All three of them are achievers, highly committed Christians, talented and gifted, friendly and loving with hosts of friends and admirers. They're great!

Our two children are doing well in their chosen vocations and we are so proud of them. We have family pictures all over our house. Each morning I look at each member of the family. I thank God for each one and pray that God will be with each one in every decision they make.

There have been difficult places in my life such as seeing Franklin through two heart attacks and quadruple by-pass heart surgery, some times of my own depression, but God has always seen me through. I've had far more good times than bad! God has given me a wonderful husband who still is the "joy of my life" and we grow closer every day. He has given me a wonderful family, good friends, and a beautiful church in which to worship and serve. The older years bring new ways of serving, but they are just as meaningful as others.

I give to God all my todays and all my tomorrows, and all my unseen future. The "longer I serve him, the sweeter he grows."

Jesus and the Children of the World

Thank you, Gertie, for this testimonial. They are not empty words—they are you life. How fortunate I am to be married, to love you, and to be loved by you. How blessed I am to be your husband.

How fortunate I am to be a member of this loving and wonderful family! Thank God for them! I cannot ever repay them for their faith in me and for encouraging me in my life as a minister.

Christ and the church have always been central to our family. Over the mantel in our living room is a most unusual painting of Jesus and children of the world. Its powerful symbolism has never been lost on our family. We have had many family worship experiences as we sat in front of a blazing fire and looked up at the painting. Jesus stands beside a boat, pulled ashore from a sparkling lake. He and a group of children are playing tug-of-war together. He is strong and could easily pull the rope from the children, but obviously he is enjoying this game; he is laughing, his teeth showing. Many ethnic children are represented in the painting—God really loves all of us! So, our family grew together, loving a God who likes us enough to laugh with us, a God who belongs to the whole world, and we all belong to him! And so we entertained—simply but joyously—people from all over the world. We grew together in global vision, in worship, in play, in relationships.

We had scores of picnics, in the backyard or in city parks; we enjoyed rich fellowship with Howard and Thelma and their daughters Beverley and Becky. We played games; we visited all sorts of places; we traveled widely. There was a striving for excellence, a high quality in living, in food, entertainment, music, art, beauty in nature, and in relationships. I am a better person because our family helped make me what I am. We've reveled in each other's successes, and wept together in pain and grief. What a marvelous creation is family! Think of cherished childhood experiences—we had them! Think of pets and dolls, friends and cousins, bicycles and skates, fishing and kite flying. Think of school plays and music lessons, the heartbreak that sometimes accompanies personal growth, the ecstasy of warm approval and showing appreciation, of answered prayers, and breathtaking worship experiences. These are all a part of our journey.

Tom is four years older than Sue. In between was Joan Esther, our stillborn daughter. Tom and Sue loved and protected each other, teased and outraged each other—all precious memories. Tom fell in love with Sandra Haynes from Wichita, Kansas, and married her two days after they both graduated from Anderson College. Sue fell in love with Spencer Spaulding, of Brookings, South Dakota, and they were married a few days after Anderson College graduation. All four are gifted, loving, and devoted Christians.

Tom and Sandy have one son, Scott, now a handsome teacher of German in Forest Grove, Oregon, who earned a Master's degree in German from Purdue University. He has studied in Germany and has traveled extensively. He is also a disciplined runner, skier, and coach. He has a talent for woodworking, and is a gifted writer and philosopher. Sandy has a Master's degree in organ performance from Wichita State University. She is a high school teacher, and director of the Oregon Children's Choir and Youth Chorale. She is a gifted organist, a professional decorator, and a gracious hostess. Tom, head of choral music at Warner Pacific College, is also Minister of Music at a Lutheran Church, director of outstanding chamber music singers, and immediate past president of the Northwest Region of American Choral Directors' Association. Tom's Doctorate is from the University of Missouri at Kansas City. Both have toured extensively with choirs in the USA, and Europe; both are gifted arrangers and composers of choral music.

Sue holds a Master's degree in early childhood education from Oakland University in Michigan and has taught in public and private schools. She is now an instructor of English at Anderson University. She is an accomplished speaker and writer, homemaker and hostess, and gifted organist. Spencer is an ordained minister and former pastor. He is now a Professor of Religious Studies at Anderson University. Spencer is a very interesting and popular preacher and teacher. He has many calls every year to teach classes or lead conferences, or preach in many churches. Spencer studied for three years at the seminary of the University of St. Andrews, Scotland. Both he and Sue are active in Park Place Church of God.

Their daughters are Gwen and Christy. Gwen is a dedicated teacher of English at Lawrence North High School in Indianapolis, and is a gifted poet and writer and charming hostess. She is married to Dr. Michael Spaulding-Barclay, a pediatric resident at James

Whitcomb Riley Children's Hospital. Gwen and Michael are loyal members of St. Luke's Methodist Church in Indianapolis.

Christy is married to Marc Boyer, from Sarasota, Florida, and both are Anderson University seniors; Christy is majoring in graphic design, and Marc in history and mathematics. As I write this, Christy is completing her internship at The Indianapolis Children's Museum.

She is also a talented ballet dancer and artist. Marc has participated in several drama productions at Anderson University, and represented Anderson University at the Model United Nations Assembly at Harvard. He is also a gourmet cook. Their son, Christoph Clay, age three, is a special child, who has made his way into the hearts of all of us. Though he suffers from Cerebral Palsy, he radiates a joy and serenity that endears him instantly to all he meets. He is a cherished, adored and doted upon great-grandchild. The Boyers attend Park Place Church of God, where many loving, praying friends surround Clay and his parents.

Both Gertie and I are the last living siblings of our families, but our family circle has been widened, and made richer by wonderful nieces, nephews, and cousins. Icy, Ocy, and Howard and their spouses are gone, but we are linked by Ocy's son, Dale Nye, and by Beverley (Pitts) and Becky (Pence) Howard and Thelma's daughters and their wonderful, expanding families. Our family has been deeply enriched by the Barclays (parents of Mike), and the Boyers (parents of Marc). How fortunate am I to be a part of this marvelous family! We join in celebration at every possible opportunity, utilizing various forms of communication (postal mail, e-mail, and voice mail) in order to stay in touch, admire, encourage, commiserate, inform, love, pray for, worship with and support one another! I am forever indebted to all these who make up our family. I can never adequately thank them or repay them for their love and compassion.

I have more time now than ever to reflect on God's mercy and redemptive love and on the gracious goodness of family. There are not many years left for me, but each moment in each hour I treasure the loving embrace of our dear family, and in the great blessings of God. Thank you all! God bless you!

II

Smile A While

In a church service somewhere in North America, the pastor referred to Jesus in the garden of Gethsemane, but he pronounced it in three syllables: Geth-se-main. He went on to say Peter "drew his sword and cut off the servant of the High Priest's ear." Can it be said in a better way? We young people who heard this later laughed hilariously!

First Days at Anderson College

When I left home in September, 1929, my father gave me thirteen dollars, all he could spare. With that and what I had managed to save, I came to Anderson College. That was an exciting year! I learned a lot—mostly in the field of extra-curricular activities. I made friendships that lasted a lifetime. A. F. Gray was pastor of Park Place Church of God; and R. L. Berry was director of the Associated Budgets, a forerunner of World Service. I wrote the winning essay in a contest on Christian stewardship. Soon after, Brother Berry offered me the job of driving his car for some long promotional trips, handling the logistics of his meetings, and a modest salary. The travel was tempting; the chance to visit many congregations, exciting; but I turned it down and continued as a student at Anderson College until the end of the school year.

What an exciting and growing year that was for me. Ruth Johnson, later to become Mrs. Coolidge, Eve Clare Holbrook (Kardatzke), Eustace Johnson, Joel Hull, and Herbert Thompson were freshmen with me. Just ahead of me in the sophomore class was my roommate and best friend, Kenneth Ahrendt. Other sophomores were Ralph Coolidge, Myrtle and Ruby Meyer, Opal Davis, and Clair Schultz.

I played the saxophone and helped to organize the first band and orchestra Anderson College ever had. Admittedly, since then, there have been a few improvements by Dale Bengston, James Rouintree, and Mark Murray, but our director was a local resident who had played with John Phillips Sousa. You should have heard us play "The Stars and Stripes Forever!" We also started the first Anderson

College orchestra; Fern Ludwig was the director of our all-male orchestra, doubtless the forerunner of the Anderson Symphony Orchestra. We organized a debate team and led the College to a two-win, two-draw season, and its first in intercollegiate debates. There were may other firsts, as well.

My life was forever enriched by many Anderson College teachers and mentors such as Amy Lopez, Earl Martin, and Dean Russell Olt, with whom I went on to share a lifetime friendship. Other mentors included J. A. Morrison, A. T. and Ida Byrd Rowe, Russell and Bessie Byrum, William and Wilma Bowser, Pastor and Mrs. E. A. Reardon, H. A. Sherwood and his wife, Walter and Ariel Haldeman, and W. E. Monk. Brother Monk was one of the most colorful of all our national church leaders.

One of my experiences at Anderson College in accepting new patterns of thought and conduct came when the stage play, *The Green Pastures* by Marc Connally, was being given in the Old English Theater in Indianapolis. Dr. Martin and Dr. Amy Lopez cancelled classes for students who wanted to go. Mrs. Rowe offered her car, as did others. This was in the days when the Church of God did not approve of theater, but a large crowd of students and our chaperones went. Tickets were expensive. Cecil Bird, David Martin, others, and I pressed for more tickets and offered to usher for free tickets, and our offer was accepted. It was hectic! I ushered in the balcony. Could my mother see me now—or my Cedar Rapids pastor!

One scene I have always remembered. It portrayed the intertestamental period of church history. Sin and evil were vividly portrayed. In the midst of all the evil, one man was seen praying to God, very intensely. Up in heaven *De Lawd* was moved by this prayer. He paced and fretted, bothered. Finally Gabriel calls out, " 'Where you goin', Lawd?" *De Lawd* said "I can't stand to hear a man pray like this. I'm goin' down to my people." And *De Lawd* put on his cloak and went down-down-down the long stairs to a barn in Bethlehem then wrapped himself up in a tiny body with no language in the night but a baby's cry. *De Lawd* came down to save his people. He answered one man's prayer for salvation. He is still there. Emmanuel—Savior. He still answers prayer. We find him on our journey—our home!

That year was a time of many new experiences. When many students left the campus to be with family or friends at Thanksgiving or Christmas, some of us who remained accepted the dinner invitations of people like Mrs. H. A. Sherwood, Mrs. Earl Martin, or Mrs. J. A. Morrison and spent the time eating and playing games. On one such weekend of vacation from classes, Kenneth Ahrendt, a few others, and I arranged an evening of a sort of talent show. I recall that I was dressed as a flirtatious young woman and actually flirted with Dean Olt. He was embarrassed and I enjoyed it.

On another weekend Rolla Shultz (brother of Clair and uncle of Pastor David Shultz) took several of us students to a frozen farm pond for ice skating. I wore leather high-tops and my old clamp on skates. I fell through the ice to my knees and did not know my feet were wet. Rolla built a small fire on the bank where I got warm and partially dry. We had a lot of fun, but when I got back to my dorm room, I found that one toe on each foot was wet and frozen! I wore soft slippers for two weeks; my toes were permanently damaged and still (seventy years later) give me problems.

Cecil Brown took the initiative to plan for athletic events. He persuaded several of us to get ready for participation in a "sports day" with Anderson High School. I am not an athlete, but Cecil was persuasive, so I exercised and trained for a couple of track events. We did not win, and it took me days to recover from aching muscles.

The college building, affectionately dubbed Old Main, was constructed with concrete blocks made on the spot, using sand from a pit just south of the building. It was used initially for lodging for the Gospel Trumpet Company workers. The building was in the shape of a huge *H,* with the east and west wings on the north side forming a large

Old Main

area that covered a large underground cistern for a holding tank for run off rain water, and near the cistern an underground coal bin. Automobile traffic coming to the front of the building used a cinder-covered driveway coming from Fifth Street. On the north side of the street was a cinder path used as a sidewalk, connecting the college building and the Gospel Trumpet Company.

During the school year the college set aside one full day as a work-day. All students, faculty, and employees were expected to be in work clothes and spend the day changing the landscaping. There were many shovels, rakes, and wheelbarrows. The assignment was to remove all the cinders from the front driveway and the path along the street, and dump them in the cistern. It was an ambitious assignment! We worked hard all day. Much of the time I pushed a wheelbarrow filled with cinders and gravel and emptied it into the cistern. We got the cistern full and some left over. In the following days an attractive rock garden with a fountain was built over the old cistern. In the

process someone lost control of his wheelbarrow and it fell crashing into the cistern. I suppose it is still there!

A favorite past time for some of us was to hike to a spot near Chesterfield. What is now University Boulevard and Third Street was the right of way then for the Interurban train. It ran from Anderson to Indianapolis at a high speed. We hiked to a place where the track crossed on a bridge over the White River, found a path leading down to the river bank, and there built a fire for a wiener roast and "burnt" marshmallows.

Freshmen were not allowed to date without special permission from the dean of students. One night I broke the rule. I took Joyce Higgins, a local high school student, to the Anderson High School gym where the Anderson College team was playing the high school in basketball. Joyce and I arrived a bit late; to find our seats we had to walk past the students and professors, and there sat Earl Martin, dean of men. He smiled at me (no permission asked or given) and did nothing about it. How foolish can a college freshman be! It was quite an eventful year for me, but it did not last long enough.

That school year began in the autumn of 1929. In chapel one day Dean Olt and President Morrison announced that the stock market had crashed. Most of us students had little idea what that meant, but we soon found out. America, and most of the rest of the world, had come to the end of an era of unbelievable prosperity, and had fallen into an abyss of financial depression almost beyond imagination. To those who were not alive to experience it, I cannot adequately describe the next few years. Despair and frustration were everywhere. Thousands committed suicide. Millions lost all of their life savings. The dark shadow of gloom and defeat allowed for no ray of hope.

At Anderson College we had started a national drive for an endowment fund. By mid-September, it had acquired the initial glow of success, but when the bottom literally fell out of the national economy, Anderson College and all other institutions were concerned only with survival. (Not even Ron Moore, nor the three Bobs: Reardon, Nicholson, and Coffman, could have helped us much then!)

In late May 1930, Dr. Morrison announced that only those students who had at least one hundred dollars in cash and whose bills were paid would be admitted if returning in September. I didn't even have a hundred pennies, and I owed the college a lot of money. So, in June, I took my broken heart and shattered dreams back to Cedar Rapids, Iowa. I had always had some kind of a job, but not this time. Millions were just like me, willing to do almost anything for a few dollars. This really was the Great Depression. I could not find any kind of job, I was broke, and I was discouraged. For me, college was out; all I wanted was survival.

III

Smile A While

Robert H. Reardon, when he was president of Anderson College, was asked to lead in prayer one night during the annual June convention. The evening service was in the Warner Auditorium. In his prayer he meant to quote from Psalm 139, "You know when I sit and when I rise." One version has it, "Thou knowest our downsitting and our uprising." Reardon's tongue slipped and he said, "Lord, thou knowest our downrisings and our upsittings." He and I lived across the street from each other, so when I saw his living room lights go on I phoned and said, "Bob, are you sure the Lord knows our downrisings and our upsittings?" He replied, "Oh, Franklin, my tongue got twisted and you don't know how embarrassed I was." We both laughed heartily. Is there a public speaker anywhere who does not know from experience how Doctor Reardon felt?

The Calling of an Evangelist

The Iowa State Camp Meeting was held at Cedar Rapids that summer of 1930. Elmer Lawson, long-time Iowa pastor, was starting a new congregation in Fort Dodge, Iowa, and asked me to preach at a tent meeting there. I hesitated, arguing that I had no previous experience preaching in tent meetings or anywhere, for that matter. He listened politely, finally won, and I went to Fort Dodge. We set up a tent, built benches, did some advertising, and began a tent meeting. I am placed in an unpayable lifetime debt to those dear people in Fort Dodge, and to thousands of others who later showed patience, love, and encouragement to my stumbling efforts in preaching. In those depression days, people went to church partly because they had no money to go elsewhere and partly for mutual support and strength from God. I know that my sermons were never profound, and I am still embarrassed when I think of my sermons in those early years. All day, and after the evening service, I studied and prayed, prayed and studied, getting ready for the next service. I had my Bible and a book by J. Grant Anderson and Russell Byrum, *Scripture Readings and Sermon Outlines*. Neither the Bible nor the book should carry the blame for what I developed from them!

Each night more people came to the tent meeting. I led the singing with my saxophone; Marjorie Lawson and I often sang duets; and I preached. Coila Bohn (Kleinhenn) was always there with her faithful parents and family.

The Lord blessed us. Twenty-four persons made commitments to him and most of them decided to be baptized on the last Sunday afternoon of the revival. It is important to note that Brother Lawson suffered greatly from sciatic rheumatism. As I reflected on it in later years, I was sure that he could turn his illness on or off at will. The Lord's Supper and foot washing were to be observed on Sunday morning. Brother Lawson insisted that I prepare to lead both, since his sciatica might prevent him from doing so. I reluctantly agreed, and we got through both experiences with a great outpouring of the Lord's Spirit. Baptism in the afternoon, though, was another matter; I tried to refuse to lead that service. Finally, though, I agreed to be prepared, just in case the rheumatism should happen to interfere again. It did, of course, and I carried on the service, baptizing twenty-one persons in the Des Moines River.

One of the converts was a rather large woman. She agreed to be baptized, but "not by that 'boy preacher'!" That was perfectly fine with me, but when the service began, she was the first candidate. I led her to the place where I had left a marker. I was very nervous. So was she. When I raised my hand to give the baptismal ritual, a marvelous peace came over the woman and me. Only a few times in later years have I had such a moving experience. It seemed to me that the Lord was stamping his validating approval upon this solemn act of ministry. I was overwhelmed and, from then on, completely at ease. Only later did I realize what risks those persons and I had taken; God blessed the total experience and I treasure that memory.

A couple of nights during those two weeks of tent meetings a pastor from nearby Madrid, Rev. Owens, paid us a visit. He was skeptical of this young preacher who had spent a year at Anderson College, but he asked me to stop and preach for his congregation on Monday night. Since Madrid was on my way home, I did. At the end of the service, he announced (without asking me) that we would have service again on Tuesday night, and so it went for more than two weeks. Paul Bengtson, who later became Opal's husband, led the singing; he and I sang a duet almost every night. The Lord blessed in spite of all human weaknesses. There were more than thirty commitments, many of them coming from young people, and most of those are still living as staunch, faithful Christians. A few years later, I was moved to learn that Paul and Opal Bengtson named their baby son, Franklin Dale.

It was still the Depression, though, and I could not get enough money to return to Anderson College. I did enroll in the correspondence program of the college and successfully completed all the course offerings.

Meantime, other calls came for revival meetings and I responded. Those evangelistic efforts took me to most of our few congregations in Iowa, to Colorado, Kansas, Oklahoma, Missouri, Indiana; later to Ohio, Massachusetts, New Hampshire, Connecticut, Vermont, New Jersey, New York, Rhode Island, Maryland, Florida, California, Texas, and Kentucky— ultimately, in fact, to all fifty states.

Later I was able to return for more studies at Anderson College but not to graduate. For employment, I worked at the Anderson newspaper office inserting sections from 1:30 A.M. to 4:30 A.M., did custodial work at the Anderson Fur Company, dishwashing in the college kitchen, cataloguing for the college library, and so on. Then I got a job at the Gospel Trumpet Company and soon became foreman of the shipping department. At Park Place Church of God, I taught senior high youth and was also the youth director. I have vivid memories of a wonderful youth group, which included Bob Reardon, Mark Bright, Joyce Byrum, Edith Gardner, Tommy Rowe, Mona Morrison, Dorothy Morrison, P. K. Padget, and many others. They profoundly enriched my life and I am still indebted to them for their gracious response to my leadership.

This was a very crucial time in my life. I was recovering from a most unfortunate romantic experience, and was in deep depression. Many close friends were most helpful, kind, and considerate, but I view it now from a new perspective. I marvel anew at the many ways God spoke to me of my need to clarify and answer my call to ministry. God, like the psalmist said, "He drew me out up from the desolate pit, out of the miry bog, and set my feet upon a rock" (Psalm 40:2, NRSV).

I recall one night when I was near the bottom of the pit, confused, and discouraged. Earlier, I referred to the old Interurban train which every hour or so moved on its tracks on which is now University Boulevard and continuing to Third Street. This one dark and dismal night I walked alone on the tracks leading toward Chesterfield and Indianapolis, and toward Jackson's Crossing of the White River. The Tempter was so real, so convincing—it was like a palpable presence. As that roaring train approached I did not need to step into the grass beside the rail—all my misery could be ended just by not moving off the track. That was really a low point in my emotions, but the Lord was there, also, and he helped me get off the track and stand in the grass berm while the speeding car rushed past. How close it was. The Lord took over, held me steady, and in a few days I was back near the center of his will and plan.

The Calling of a Pastor

I recall that shortly after that Doctor Rowe, general manager of the publishing house, called me into his office for a fatherly talk. He told me about the efforts of the Board of Church Extension and Home Missions many years before when they were trying to establish congregations in certain strategic urban areas. They had done this in Atlanta, Omaha, Portland, Oregon, Houston, and Boston. None had been an outstanding success, but all still had the nucleus of a new congregation of the Church of God. Earl Martin had been sent to Boston, Massachusetts and had successfully started two Sunday schools and one congregation in the suburban city of Everett. Steele Smith was there now and having considerable success in saving the struggling church. Steele was leaving, coming to Anderson to work for the national Board of Church Extension in investment counseling. That would leave the Everett church without a pastor. Dr. Rowe made it clear that my work at the Gospel Trumpet Company was quite satisfactory, but he felt I should be in a place where my gifts could be used in pastoral leadership.

I earnestly sought divine guidance and felt I should go. It was all arranged. I went. I preached. The people warmly welcomed me and invited me to become their pastor. I accepted! The people really loved Steele and his charming wife, Grace, but if the church could not keep them, they thought I might do alright as second best! Anyway, I accepted and stayed in the Boston area. The following years were a time of hard work and growth for me. God was leading me in new aspects of my journey. God's Spirit seemed to bless the entire arrangement.

Still today, Helen Martin Shoemaker and I can compare memories of life in what was both church and parsonage at 79 Bucknam Street in Everett, Massachusetts, where her father, Earl Martin, had begun this congregation many years earlier. The Boston days were difficult but rewarding. My brother, Howard, soon joined me there, found employment, and assisted me in so many ways in the work of the church. I cannot say how deeply I appreciate his help, both as brother and as friend and co-worker. It was there that he met Thelma Anderson, who became his lovely bride and companion in ministry.

I had already met, in a casual way, Gertie Andrew, a senior at Anderson College. I now felt that I should pursue her in a more than casual manner.

IV

Gertie Andrew sang in the Anderson College Ladies Quartet, and I had admired her greatly. She had all the beauty, personality, talent,

Anderson College Quartet: Gertie Andrews, first on the left

and attributes one could want, but she was also seriously dating an Anderson College man who could *really* sing; it even made my heart quiver when they sang "The Indian Love Call." With some gentle conspiracy from Glenyce Sayer, Esther Boyer, and a few others, I was able to break up that unfortunate romance and persuade Gertie to give some attention to me. After her graduation from Anderson, she became youth and music director of the Church of God in Baltimore, Maryland. That made my quest easier.

Our wedding was in the Baltimore church. At our wedding Pastor L. T. Flynt read the ceremony. Glenyce Sayre, Gertie's roommate in college and a dear friend, was the maid of honor. My brother was the best man. The Baltimore congregation just over-whelmed us with their thoughtful and kind preparation for the wedding—down to the smallest detail and a lavish reception following. The congregation in Boston raised my salary from ten dollars to fifteen dollars per week. The next few years in New England were difficult, even poverty-filled, but also delightful and precious in pastoral experiences.

In Boston, we had many visitors from Anderson, some on business-related trips and some just to see us (at least we thought so). We enjoyed hosting Harold Phillips, Ida Byrd Rowe, Nora Angus, Lottie Franklin, Dean Russell Olt, Steele Smith, Earl Martin, Elver Adcock, and many others. These visitors always enriched our lives, and we were, and are, so very grateful. During the war years we entertained many military persons—all the Church of God chaplains, many sailors, soldiers, marines, and many wives and sweet hearts. We gladly entertained them all; how my dear wife did it, on our salary of fifteen dollars a week, I really do not know, but she entertained royally and everyone enjoyed it.

The New England days were difficult because we had little money for any thing more than actual expenses, but we were in love (and still are, after sixty-two years) and the Lord opened many doors for witnessing and for service.

I obtained names and addresses of every person in New England who had had any contact with any of our national church agencies. I wrote to them; often Gertie and I (later with Tommy) visited dozens of them. This opened doors for expanding ministries—preaching, weddings, funerals, starting new congregations, writing, encouraging, dreaming, praying, and working hard.

This is being written in May 2000. Just a couple of months ago I received a beautiful card from a couple whose wedding vows I led sixty years ago! It was a moving memory. One of the women who had been led to the Lord in that New Hampshire meeting came to me in tears one day in the Boston parish. Her daughter was pregnant. Would I perform this wedding ceremony? Of course I would! There wasn't much time for counseling then—it came later, but in our little apartment, there was a wedding. Gertie served coffee and cookies, but, in the midst of this sweet, tiny wedding reception, the newly married couple had to hurry to the delivery room of a nearby hospital. Now, sixty years later, they are a family happy and in love by the grace of God and still serving him. That was a priceless experience.

So many names could be given—scores we led to the Lord. We loved our work, and lasting friendships were formed there. The New England years were great years for Gertie, Tommy, and me.

The summer following our marriage, Gertie and I went to Rochester, New Hampshire, Sunday through Friday for three weeks, spending only Saturday night and Sunday morning at our congregation in Massachusetts. We rented a vacant Unitarian Church building for four dollars a week (our own money), led a vacation Bible school in the day time, visited, sang and preached; there were some converts and some baptisms in a beautiful New England lake. My brother, Howard, became the pastor of this small group and the church there is still active today. We helped start other congregations, and I preached in all six New England states. We started a youth camp with Dean Olt as visiting leader, on property owned by Mrs. Anna Blewitt. It was successful. Norma Blewitt Eikamp, her sister, Joyce, Robert Smith (later a Pennsylvania pastor), Thelma Anderson Miller, Ruby and Charles Clark (sister and brother of Evelyn Clark Clear), and

many others came out of those days of ministry. Florence Harvey was a vivacious member of that youth group, and she found Ward Jackson while I was there; I married them. Gertie and I were so happy in our New England ministries. Our son, Tom, was born there; I completed my college degree at Gordon College and took other studies at some of the highly respected universities. We had no money, but we had many values money cannot buy.

I was now pastor of a congregation of the Church of God in greater Boston, where Martin Anderson was chairperson of the board and leader of the Sunday morning worship. I was accustomed to planning and leading worship. So was he. For a while he and I worked together without friction, then we both found there was an estrangement between us. It grew worse every

day. All of our people saw it. We hardly spoke to each other. This was hurting my preaching and leadership; Martin had many friends and a lot of relatives in the church. We had trouble. Some suggested that, as pastor, I should take the initiative and clear our misunderstandings. Gertie suggested this. She and many others were praying. Then the Holy Spirit led me to see I should show some leadership. I did.

The next Sunday I talked to Martin and said I was to blame for our situation. He said he was and we spent some time each trying to take the blame. Finally he asked me to have dinner at his home the next day and afterwards we talked. He reminded me that he was the chairperson of the board; I, instead of he, had given permission for a building contractor to run a sewer line across the church property and connect with a manhole on our property. Martin felt that I was thus usurping his authority, and I had no business granting such permission. He was right; I was wrong. I finally said so and apologized.

We embraced each other, Martin forgave me; we wept a little and smiled a lot and were reconciled in the spirit of Christian love. He became my close friend and was my strong ally for the rest of his life. I learned that a true Christian will sometimes have to "eat humble pie" regardless of who was right or wrong. I learned that unity is more important than self-satisfaction and not many things are important enough to break unity and fellowship. The community of faith is larger than our self interests and must be preserved.

Our journey in the New England days was influenced so much by many of the persons who entered our lives; not all of them can be named; however, it is important to name some of them.

Ted Johnson

Early in our ministry we met Ted Johnson, a Swedish-American who lived in Malden. Ted played the piano quite well. He also had a beautiful tenor voice. Ted had been divorced. When we met him he was married to Ella. She was vivacious, charming, of average beauty, not a musician. Ted frequently played the piano for our Sunday services, and often sang a solo or a duet with Gertie, my wife. After a few months Ted was named our music leader (without pay) and assumed leadership of a voluntary choir.

In the early autumn of 1939, Ted suggested that we could unite our choir with that of one or more nearby churches and present a Christmas concert. We obtained the enthusiastic support of singers from the nearby Church of Christ, and some others from the Mystic Side Congregational Church. Ted, a tenor, and my wife Gertie, a lyric soprano, were the only ones with vocal training. Gertie had sung extensively as a member of the Anderson College Ladies Quartet and had studied at Baltimore's Peabody Conservatory. Music copies were obtained and weekly rehearsals began with Ted conducting from the piano. We were not in competition with the Boston Symphonic Choir or anyone else; we sang for the sheer joy of it and to the glory of God. Ted arranged for us to sing selections from Handel's *Messiah*. This was really quite ambitious for us, but the December concert and little church building was filled with friends and loyal supporters. It was really quite well done. I was proud of us. Ted and Gertie in the months ahead frequently sang duets, always beautifully done and enthusiastically received.

Ted and Ella were among our close friends. He was a member of the Maplewood-Malden Swedish Methodist Church, but he and Ella became regular leaders in the Everett-Malden Church of God. They gave a strong witness to God. They brought great joy on the journey!

Margaret Malemezian was Armenian, crippled enough that she always walked with a visible limp. She had been with the Everett-Malden congregation since its early days. Her husband, Sarkis, had a printing business in downtown Boston. They lived in Dorchester which for Mrs. Malemezian was a fifty minute train ride by surface car, then the elevated and subway train. Only in severely inclement weather did she miss one of our church services. Gertie and I enjoyed having dinner with her and her husband. Her specialty was Yaprach Dolma, an Armenian entree of ground lamb and beef seasoned and rolled in processed grape leaf, then cooked to near perfection. In our mid-week Bible study Mrs. Malemezian always brought new insights from the Armenian Bible. When her husband died I participated in the memorial service, along with the minister of the Orthodox Church and officials from the lodge of which Sarkis was a member.

When Mrs. Malemezian later moved to an apartment, she sold us some of the furniture which is now owned by our son Dr. Thomas and his wife Sandra who have the classic sofa; and Marc and Christy Boyer who have the mahogany table and chairs. We have the enduring memories of Mrs. Malemezian.

Julian Laughlin and his wife lived in Barnet, Vermont—a picture book Yankee village, complete with the white Congregational Church clear glass windows, full steeple, village green, covered bridge, and a country store. Julian operated the store and was the town printer and postmaster. He and his wife lived on the first floor of a two-flat house, and his sister Robina lived by herself in the second floor apartment. I knew Julian mostly by reputation, not through personal acquaintance. He had intense loyalty to the Church of God. He had several life loan notes with the national Board of Church Extension and Home Missions. He had a standing order with the Gospel Trumpet Company (now Warner Press) for one copy of each of their new publications and a lifetime subscription to the *Gospel Trumpet.*

While we were still in New England Julian became ill and died. Dr. Adcock, treasurer of the Board of Church Extension, asked me to informally represent them in an effort to get Mrs. Laughlin to relinquish rights to their investments of loans or to name her sister-in-law Robina Laughlin a contingent beneficiary. Because a Vermont attorney had already contacted Julian's widow, it was deemed inadvisable for an officer or even a full member of the Board of Church Extension to enter the state of Vermont and be subject to certain legal procedures. I went and did my best, but it was too late. The attorney, a Barnet lawyer, had already obtained other agreements from Mrs. Laughlin. She lived only a short while after the death of her husband.

A short while later, Miss Robina Laughlin, Julian's sister, invited me to visit her. My brother went with me. I was pleasantly surprised on meeting Robina. She was handicapped and rarely left the apartment for any reason. I found her living room lined floor to ceiling with bookshelves, all filled with the classics and her religious and fiction books. She had read most of them.

She listened regularly by short-wave radio to news broadcasts and programs from all over the world. She was mentally keen and alert, and knowledgeable of world events and personalities. What an enriching day Howard and I spent with Miss Robina.

She gave me a small hand-operated printing press and about twenty fonts of movable type and other personal mementos from her late brother Julian.

Howard had borrowed a truck and a driver. We put the small press on the truck and tied it down with ropes, and traveled through the Vermont Hills and New Hampshire's mountains to Massachusetts. I used the press for about three years for printing a monthly paper we call *The New Englander*, mailing about four hundred copies. When we moved to Indiana I had the printing equipment with me and finally gave it to Warner Press to set up in their lobby as an interesting exhibit. Robina gave us a memorable visit on that part of our journey.

Miss Nellie Laughlin, a sister of Robina and Julian, had never married and was now retiring from a lifetime of missionary service to Egypt and Lebanon under the Church of God Missionary Board. I knew her only by reading missionary literature, until after I met her in New York City.

The New York City Church of God met in the "Missionary Home," where Miss Axchie Bolitho was pastor. She and her mother supervised the Missionary Home in the Bronx as a sort of "guest house." At the invitation of Miss Bolitho, I was speaker for a one-week preaching mission. Present for the first Sunday of the preaching was Miss Nellie Laughlin. She had with her a close friend, a woman from North Carolina. After the evening service I was going upstairs to my room when Miss Laughlin saw me and called for my attention. She said firmly, "It has been at least thirty years since I saw Times Square at midnight, and my friend and I want you to escort us down there tonight." I gave a mild protest and some excuses because I also was a stranger in New York City, but to no avail. So off we went, with a few general suggestions from our hostess, Miss Bolitho. We walked a short distance to the subway station and managed to get on an express train. It was fast, but did not stop at the station where we were supposed to change trains, so we had to take a slower local train back, and after a couple more similar changes and connections we got to the famous Times Square. In those days that area was relatively safe and free from crime. We took in all the sights, ate a snack, and at last got on another subway train bound for the Bronx and "home." Again we managed to get on an express train that moved right through our station stop to change trains; again we spent an hour or so getting the correct train to the Bronx station. It was past three o'clock in the morning, but as we walked toward our destination, Miss Laughlin called out in delight as she passed a restaurant still open, with an attractive window sign inviting us to come in and enjoy a kosher pastrami sandwich. "T. Franklin," she called, "I have not tasted such a sandwich for almost forty years, and I would like to have one now." In we went and we all indulged with delight. We got to our rooms after four o'clock in the morning. How could I ever forget the Laughlin family from Vermont, Egypt, and Lebanon! What joy we have now in recalling memories such as these!

Dot and Fred Lunn

There were other persons who brought interest and excitement on our journey in New England—such as the Lunn family. It began when we met Dot one evening at the home of Ted and Ella Johnson. Her name was Dorothy but Ella called her Dot. So, that is what we called her. That first evening she was cold and non-committal. Usually we got only a "yes" or "no" or a nod of her head. She definitely was warmer to Gertie and to Ella than she was to me or to Ted. She seemed to carry and nourish a hatred for men. In a later meeting she had her niece, Bunny, with her. It took several meetings, lots of patience, and considerable tact, but gradually we got acquainted. She lived alone in an apartment; her mother and a brother lived in another apartment and they did not often communicate with each other. Dot had membership in the big Boston Tremont Temple Baptist Church, but had little respect for any church and never attended services there. She was a chain smoker of cigarettes. She worked in the editorial offices of the Malden daily newspaper. One Sunday she came to our church with Ella, but left without speaking to anyone.

Through Ted and Ella, Dot learned that we were hoping soon to construct a new church building and that we wanted very much to acquire some land on Main Street, Malden, just a block from the town of Everett. The lots we wanted were a part of an estate, still in litigation settlement. It included a large plot of land of about thirty or more building lots, plus the land we wanted of about ten building lots. The banker and owner would not even discuss it with us. It was our hope that the Board of Church Extension would provide loans that would enable us to buy the land some day in the future. All of this Dot knew, but she was still cool toward me.

One day Steele Smith of the Board of Church Extension was visiting us on church business, discussing the future of the Everett-Malden Church. About ten o'clock Dot Lunn called to say, quite cryptically but showing some interest, that the people representing the big estate on Main Street would be in session at 2:00 o'clock the next day at the Malden Trust Company. She could get an appointment for us if we had someone available who could speak with authority on the sale of the property. I gave her the needed information and she got an appointment for Dr. Smith. There would be other bidders, but she and we were still hopeful.

Steele went to the meeting. He entered a bid of $5,000.00 for the lots on Main Street, about six of them, one hundred and fifty feet deep. They were on the route of the bus feeder line to the elevated train station, connecting Malden Square with quick access to the rapid transit trains. Steele's bid was accepted.

We felt the Lord was directing this move and boldly began the next step, the building process. This meant getting a capable architect, raising funds, and making plans to remodel the Seventy-nine Bucknam Street property in Everett. What great rejoicing we had. I called Dot Lunn to thank her for the hot tip, and she grudgingly said she would do it for anyone.

Dot Lunn gradually warmed toward me and others. I learned that she had once been a Girl Scout leader; after proper consultation with others in the church, we formed a Girl Scout Troop with Dot Lunn as the leader. One day she confided in Gertie and me the full story. She had an affair with an unnamed man and became pregnant with Bunny, her "niece"—really her daughter. We helped her find relief in her confession, then led her gently to a new and deeper commitment of her life to God. She became a charming woman and a good friend. Later she and a man named Henry became good friends and agreed to be married. I was to perform the ceremony in our apartment. Gertie prepared tea and cookies. Dot felt she should confess the whole story to Henry, which she did before I began the ceremony. Henry listened with patience, then said, "Mr. Miller, I have the marriage license and I think everything is in order. We are ready if you are." So they were married. In due time Henry adopted "Bunny." When I last heard, they were all still happy. Dot was won by patience, trust, and redemptive love.

That was a celebrative event in our faith pilgrimage but there is more. Dot had a brother, Fred. His story was one of our earliest encounters, after he had come to one of our Sunday morning services. He had been a strong Christian and a member of the Tremont Temple Baptist Church in Boston. He fell in love with a beautiful woman who appeared to be dedicated to high ideals as a Christian. After a year or so of marriage, she became restless and began suggesting that Fred take her to dances. He did. Then he started to smoke cigarettes as she did. They gradually indulged with friends in social drinking—a first for Fred. He learned that he was an alcoholic and could not resist the cocktails. His wife divorced him and he went back to live in the apartment with his mother. Almost every week he got drunk. He still attended our church services when he was sober. I patiently treated him with kindness, always praying that surrounding him with redemptive love would lead to his conversion.

Late one night Mrs. Lunn, Fred's mother, called me in great distress. Fred had come home drunk and had fallen to the floor of the vestibule and she could not get him up to their room. I went to help and, gradually, with a neighbor's help, we got Fred upstairs and on the sofa. We let him sleep. I left for a couple of hours, then returned and sat with him until he was awake. His mother and I got some food and some strong coffee into him and finally he was sober enough to show shame and regret. Later he apologized to me for his behavior. Patience and redemptive love finally won and there came a day when Fred confessed his sins, received God's forgiveness, and was converted. I took him to several meetings of Alcoholics Anonymous and stayed reasonably close to him for months. He was able to find employment and remained sober. Diagnosed with a brain tumor, he became ill and was a patient in the Veteran's hospital nearby. Later as Gertie and I were preparing to move to Anderson, Indiana, I received from Fred a long handwritten letter of gratitude for helping him become a new man in Christ. There are many rewards that came unsolicited in our journey of faith!

The Andersons

One or two more stories must be told. Frank and Mary Anderson had a long and blessed history of supporting the work of the Lord; they had no children but treated me as a son. One day they took me to the furniture store of Clifford and Black in Malden, selected solid maple twin beds, and bought them for me. We are still using them after more than sixty years. Frank was the church treasurer, always pained that my salary was so low. When Gertie and I were seriously courting, I talked with Frank about getting an engagement ring. He was employed at a loan company, a sort of dignified pawn shop. Most of their clients were wealthy and dignified people who occasionally borrowed money using expensive jewelry or silver as collateral. Some items were never reclaimed and could be sold. Frank made inquiry and one day brought for my examination a beautiful diamond ring and with Frank's help, in my price range. I bought it. Gertie still wears it with her wedding ring—after sixty-five years.

Frank and Mary Anderson were solid Christians, dear, dear friends, loyal supporters of the work of the Lord. The same was true of Frank's brother, Carl Anderson, his wife, and their sister, Marie Johnson. Such memories are too precious to perish!

The Lee Family

One last story—this about the Lee family. Harry Lee was employed at the Everett Coke Plant. He was a rather blustery fellow, in his own way kind and supportive, as was his wife, Laura. They were always fluctuating up and down in their spiritual pilgrimage. They needed a lot of redemptive love and patience, and I tried as a pastor to supply that. Their older son, Newton, responded to what guidance I was able to supply especially in his late teenage years. He enlisted in the United States Navy and was accepted for submarine duty. The last letter I received from him came in the emotionally tumultuous days of his adolescence. God had used some in the church fellowship to help provide the care and stability that was lacking in the family atmosphere. Thank God for the opportunities for loving service that comes on the journey in unexpected places!

To list more of such persons as these could fill a another book. These stories are written in God's library. I regret I cannot tell them all here in this limited space, but I gratefully respect and salute their memory.

The Big Move to Anderson, Indiana

On one of his visits to Boston, Dr. Elver Adcock, executive of the National Board of Church Extension and Home Missions, invited me to become his associate as secretary of home missions. This was tempting to one with a long time interest in missionary work, but it was hard to leave our growing congregation. We now had a building, small but beautiful, four hundred on our mailing list, and a constituency of around one hundred loyal, dedicated, and loving people. To leave was difficult, but we did. We moved to Anderson.

When we left the Boston area in June, I had taken Gertie and Tommy to Federalsburg, Maryland for them to spend much of the summer with Gertie's family on the farm. Tommy was at once captured by all the family and enjoyed it. Gertie's brothers patiently helped Tommy get acquainted with the farm. It was a delightful experience for the whole family.

I went on to Anderson, Indiana and my new assignment with the Board of Church Extension and Home Missions. We stored our furniture in a down town building owned by the board and I roomed with Elver and Annabelle Adcock until Gertie could come at the end of the summer.

Many adjustments had to be made to this new life. Gertie was no longer the pastor's wife; I had to adjust to a new and more promotional preaching style, and I had to travel all over the country. Travel became synonymous with my work for the rest of my life. To Gertie fell the heavy responsibility of a growing family, plus the constant care of my mother, who came to live with us soon after we moved to Anderson, staying for the remaining eighteen years of her life. I am sure that the Lord has special stars placed in Gertie's crown, for her patience, tender loving care, and for her uncomplaining radiant life of service. With all that she carried at home, she still managed to continue singing in choirs, solos, or trios; she taught a Sunday school class, served as a department principal, wrote curriculum materials and often traveled with me. (Bless you, Darling, for your devotion and love, and for making our house a home.)

V

Our daughter Sue Miller Spaulding wrote a beautiful tribute to Gertie; I thought it appropriate to include it here.

My Mother's Beauty
By Sue Miller Spaulding

"Age cannot wither her, nor customs stale her infinite variety"
—Shakespeare

A cluster of beautiful, delicate pink roses blooms beneath my mother's sewing room window. That shadowed spot is brightened by the gentle grace of those roses; their velvety petals even cheer the darkened earth, once they've fallen to the ground. My seventy-five year old mother helps tend the cold earth; each thing my mother touches seems to become more alive, more vivid, more beautiful.

My mother's special gift of creating beauty is evident in what would otherwise be the most ordinary ways. Flamboyant, bombastic expressions of love would not suit her gentle, gracious manner. Her gift is in turning the ordinary into celebration, the plain into beautiful, the simple into abundance. A simple meal around my mother's dining room table becomes a work of beauty with her artistic touches. The fare may be modest—perhaps a simple casserole accompanied by salad and muffins, but my mother will make it seem a feast: ivory lace cloth beneath the finest china dishes, ice tinkling in crystal glasses and garnished with a sprig of mint just picked from her herb garden, candles aglow, gleaming silver, warm homemade muffins alongside her own special homemade jam, a fragrant rose bouquet as a centerpiece. What guest would not feel like royalty?

My mother is a nurturer and a nourisher. She is so loving and caring that everything touched by her seems to grow stronger and

healthier, happier and more beautiful. When she is around, violets bloom, tomatoes grow, geraniums blossom, peach trees produce, babies laugh, children thrive, bread is baked, food is served, guests are tended to, beds are clean and inviting, music is played, flowers are arranged; in short, my mother knows how to love.

Whether she is on her knees planting pansies on a spring morning, putting up peaches on a hot summer day, preparing her nearly world-famous apple pies on some glorious September afternoon, or serving tea in front of a cozy fire on a frozen winter night, my mother is forever creating, beautifying, loving, giving, in some of the most creative and graceful ways.

Sue Miller

Sometimes she even seems to create something out of what appears to be nothing at all. A sparse room comes alive with fresh, fragrant flowers; overly ripe bananas are magically turned into the most delicious banana bread; rainy afternoons and idle hours are used to compose interesting letters or fill grandchildren's scrapbooks; even a few spare moments might be spent sitting at her piano, singing in her still-clear soprano voice.

Sometimes my mother shows up unexpectedly at my door with a special surprise: a pot of stew, a loaf of bread, or a tin of her wonderful chocolate chip cookies. Just a brief visit from her leaves my family feeling better. Her quick laughter, encouraging words and hugs all around to granddaughters, daughter and son-in-law will brighten the whole rest of the day.

Perhaps other women have earned more money, or received greater fame and accolades, but no other woman could ever be as successful at life's most important job of loving, as my own, gentle, beautiful mom, Gertie M. Miller.

Thank you, Sue, you have said it so well, far better then I can, and it is all so true. I am proud to be her husband and your father.

VI

Back to Anderson—I had to find a place for us to live. That was not easy. The Board of Church Extension owned a house at 305 Ruddle Avenue and offered to rent it to me. I accepted. What furniture we had stored was placed there. I engaged painters to paint all the kitchen walls and ceiling white and do some other painting throughout the house. Twice while the men were there they told me the house had cockroaches; I had no previous experience with those delightful creatures so I was not bothered very much. The men completed the painting and one evening I went in and saw what the painters meant. It was disgusting! I was told that burning sulfur candles would destroy the pests, so I did that. Not only were some of the pests destroyed, all the white paint was now a sickly yellow color. I had it all repainted!

I discovered that house was not clean. The former tenants had kept chickens in the basement! What a mess I found, but I cleaned everything, and within a reasonable time I was able to get Gertie and Tommy, and we set about living in Anderson. Gertie and I began to make what changes we could afford and we thought would help. Later, Dr. Earl Martin, president of the board, suggested that we buy the house. He even arranged to accept all the rent we had paid as part of the sale. Not everybody was happy with this, but thanks to Dr. Martin's superb leadership and influence, he prevailed.

Dr. A. T. Rowe was then General Manager of Gospel Trumpet Company and one day he talked to me about getting a new house. The Company owned many lots and was trying to sell them. This was part of their heritage from the former leaders of the Company. He gave me lists of available lots, and Gertie and I looked at most of them. We found three adjoining lots at 1210 East Seventh Street and talked with Dr. Rowe. He would sell all three for $1500.00, less an employee discount of $200.00. I said that was most generous, but we didn't have any money. He then offered them on contract and told me to write the contract. I offered fifteen dollars down and ten dollars a month; he agreed. I wrote small articles for the *Young People's Friend,* which Mrs. Rowe edited, and I placed all the royalties on our land contract (sometimes one dollar and ninety-six cents, sometimes two dollars or more), and also the small checks I got for speaking engagements. In time, it all added to a few hundred dollars, and one day Gertie and I decided that this year we would pay the balance due on the lots. It was not easy, but we did. Then we talked with Russell Byrum, who was building new houses. We found that the government was on our side; they would loan 90 percent of the cost of a new house and the lots could be used as the down payments. At the time I was giving supply leadership at a small Presbyterian church near Anderson, and that twenty dollars a week was just enough more to make us eligible for an FHA loan. We signed a contract with Mr. Byrum and the building began. We were buying with lots of faith and little reality, but we went right on. For example, Mr. Byrum called to say the garage we planned was too small. I knew that but also knew we could not afford to add one more dollar to the cost. Undaunted, he asked if my wife drove the car; she did. He said that was reason enough to add a couple of feet to the garage. The same process happened with most of the rest of the house. When the FHA inspector made his last inspection, he asked me if I knew we were getting much more house than it was costing.

My work as secretary of home missions was challenging. I raised money to start both the Pioneer Loan Fund and the Nora Hunter Revolving Loan Fund. I guided in the opening of the Indian Mission at Crow Agency, Montana, and at Lapwai, Idaho. Assisted by Naomi Randall, I was involved in the work on the Pine Ridge, South Dakota and Tulalip, Washington reservations. I assisted in the planting of new churches in the newly congested areas around military installations and defense industries—and they were forming all over the country. I had the opportunity to place and supervise missionary workers in two of the Japanese-American Relocation Centers. Recruiting and placing migrant workers was also part of my assignment. I edited the Home Missions Board magazine, *The Pioneer*. I recruited Naomi Randall to give full-time leadership to many aspects of Home missions, especially with ministry to Appalachia. Naomi and I selected and dedicated the land upon which Pine Crest Center would eventually be built.

Two persons who enriched my life and ministry in this venture were Leland and Evelyn Harriman, then home missionaries on the

Tulalip Reservation. Evelyn's mother was the distinguished Washington pastor, Mrs. Mina Jarrett.

There were many adjustments I had to make. I was accustomed to being the pastor, the leader, and the main decision-maker. I was now a new employee, taking directions from people who had years of experience in work that was very new to me. Marie Meyer and Leona Tussey each did some of my secretarial work. This was new to me. I had to learn how best to use the services of a trained and efficient secretary. It was not easy for me, but I am sure it was much more difficult for Marie and Leona and others in the office. They were all patient and kind and helped this slow learning new-comer.

My travels started almost immediately. I had an early assignment to attend the annual meeting of the Home Missions Council of North America as the new Church of God representative. The setting was so beautiful. We met in a large resort hotel at the lakeshore at Silver Bay in upstate New York.

Mrs. Norman Vincent Peale was president of the Home Missions Council. For this conference, Dr. Mark Dawber was the worship leader. I attended every session and talked with many people about their work. It was invigorating and mind-stretching and I loved it.

I observed that Dr. Dawber frequently quoted from the Book of Psalms. One day I engaged him in conversation as we walked along the shore. In his younger days at church he had been required to memorize *all* one hundred fifty chapters of the Book of Psalms. I could not comprehend that, but it did light a fire of interest in the Psalms, and to this day I still read and study them with great interest. That week at Silver Bay was a marvelous open door for me in my new assignment in home missions. I thank God for that wonderful week.

In addition I had extended conversation with A. T. Maciel regarding future work with the Spanish-Americans; began a ministry to the African-Americans in the south; prepared printing materials for promoting giving to Home missions—and preached almost every Sunday! I was challenged by the size of the task and became intensely interested in those whom I supervised. My colleagues and associates in the office were cordial, friendly, and helpful.

Another aspect of the work was recruiting and placing persons to serve in the ministry to migrant workers, and there were many such opportunities. Some college students were placed in ministry to summer migrant workers. One outstanding person was an Anderson College student by the name of Arthur Eikamp. He was not a novice. Earlier, on his own initiative, he did volunteer work with migrant families who were harvesting tomatoes in Indiana. Later Arthur married Norma Blewitt, one of our own New England youth campers from New York. They had a most beautiful and rewarding ministry as career missionaries for Japan. What surprises come to us on the journey of life which is our home!

Someone introduced me to Naomi Randall. She was a public school teacher in Kentucky, now within one year of her lifetime certification and pension. She surrendered that to give full time to ministry to the evident needs in Appalachia, and it was a significant and rewarding ministry. She and I selected and dedicated the land on which the Pine Crest Center would eventually be located. Two others of my good friends, Simon and Mae Robinson, in later years gave generously of their energies in this ministry to Appalachia.

During World War II there were intense negative feelings toward persons of Japanese ancestry, especially on the West Coast. The United States government decided to move all such persons to "relocation centers" for the duration of the war. They are long since closed, but they are a part of an *unbelievable* stain in American life. These centers were places for prisoners of war. People were housed in old army barracks and the whole area surrounded with barbed wire and guards with live ammunition. The people had little time for preparation before being taken from the homes and were allowed one small travel case for each person. One organization that was especially active in this relocation effort was the Native Sons of the Golden West. There were other similar groups, all moved with suspicion, hatred for "foreigners," and fear.

They were taken from their homes and business establishments under guard by train to the centers. The one with which I became most familiar was a few miles from LaJunta, Colorado, in the desert. There was no regard for one's standing in the community or business association. These Japanese-Americans were doctors, dentists, teachers, lawyers, and farmers; they were highly regarded in their community and even loved by their friends and neighbors. It was not unusual for some of these friends to assume control of the business that was being left behind and care for it until the owners eventually returned.

Through the efforts of several inter-denominational agencies, permission was granted to some church groups to provide a ministry of teaching and preaching, always under strict supervision. The Church of God was allotted permission for three workers in one center. This was under my supervision. I worked through a lot of government red tape but was successful in placing Mae Johnson, EvaJoy Smith, and Mrs. S. J. Lane. We paid their travel, living expenses, and a modest salary. The work was not easy. The residents were always polite, but underneath were deep feelings of anger, resentment, and disappointment at being treated as prisoners of war when they had such excellent records of being loyal citizens.

A part of my job was to visit our three workers on location, try to discover their needs, and if possible take care of them. I was really their supervisor. On one of my visits, our three "missionaries" and I were invited for a noon luncheon at the home of one of the residents. What feelings of anger and outrage we had when we went to the door and saw there an American flag and five gold stars. This family had five sons who had been killed while serving in the United States Army. When we sat at the table, I was asked to give the prayer of thanks. That was one of the most difficult tasks I ever had. I am glad to say that some attempt has been made by Congress to apologize and redress the wrong, but nothing can blot out the bitter memories of those good people who were victims of fear, prejudice, and false values.

Dr. Adcock and I had been long-time friends but tensions were developing between us. It bothered me. From the vantage point of advanced years (I am now ninety-three-years-old), I look back and realize I was as much to blame as anyone. I was eager to take more initiative in my interpretation of my title, "Secretary of Home Missions." I can now see more of Dr. Adcock's position. Much of the work he had started and had supervised. He knew first hand all that I was just now learning. I guess the crisis was when he called L. T. Flynt to go to Alaska. The two of them spent a week or more discussing the new assignment and I didn't know anything about it. I was secretary of Home missions. The tension got worse and I resigned—not knowing where I could go or what I would do.

VII

Smile A While

I was preaching in an afternoon service in a tent at Payne, Ohio, and had arranged to leave immediately at the close of the message in order to drive approximately one hundred miles south for another speaking engagement. Our six-year-old son, Tom was with me, and sat by the front door ready to leave when I did. We got in the car right away and had driven maybe ten minutes when Tom broke the silence, "Well, Daddy, did you flop or did you wow them?" I had no quick answer, but what a question. What preacher has not often asked himself that same question.

To The Board of Christian Education

Dr. Carl Kardatzke, chair of the national Board of Christian Education of the Church of God, phoned us with a welcome surprise asking me to be the new executive secretary of Christian education. It was a surprise because it came the day after I resigned my position as secretary of home missions with the Board of Church Extension and Home Missions. I was married, had a family, and no prospect of employment. It was a welcome call, an answer to our prayers.

I did not accept at once; instead, I reminded Dr. Carl that I had neither training nor experience in the field. He simply replied that I could learn. I agreed and quickly set about learning the new assignment.

As if the career and financial crises were not enough, we had also gone through the grief of losing a baby girl. God gave us another, our lovely daughter, Sue. It was time for rebuilding and renewing. I took the position, at least for a year, and stayed at the Board of Christian Education for over twenty-two years. During this time, I traveled extensively, but, still our growing family remained closely-knit. Gertie, a loving and nurturing mother and patient wife, gets the credit for that! Christian education was unpopular with many of our pastors, so I set out to win their support and the Lord helped me get it. This called for even more travel, more promotion, more new, inventive ways to encourage and stimulate teachers and other church workers. When it was possible to do so, I took Gertie, Tom, and Sue with me, and we have traveled over the country as a family. I preached in over 1300 Church of God congregations, in all fifty states, and in more than fifty countries. I was able to attend and speak at all of our major state, area, Christian education meetings, and youth conventions within that twenty-two year span, and at many ministers' meetings and camp meetings (as well as more than my share of the minor ones, too). There was heavy involvement in interdenominational events. I chaired various committees of the International Council of Religious Education, later a part of the National Council of Churches. Lasting friendships were made there with some of the finest Christians one could ever find, many of them the great national or world leaders in their own denominations.

Christian Education and Camping

There was a wave of interest in family camping as a part of Christian education. Our family was invited to work with the Oregon Board of Christian Education, so the family went. Lorin Myer, a local director of Christian education, was also chair of the state board and director of their family camp. The plan was that Gertie and Sue would stay in Portland with friends, Tom and Clara Smith and John and Margaret Smith, while our son Tom and I would join James Wade for a week of fishing and return the following week for the family camp.

James (Jim) Wade was pastor of the Holladay Park Church of God in Portland and was a trained and experienced family counselor. Jim was also an experienced leader for outdoor activities. He handled horses well, knew camping, was an excellent camp cook, a fisherman, and hunter. He was about five foot eight inches tall, lean with a trim figure, a ruddy complexion, and engaging smile. He was an able preacher, an astute businessman, and a friendly guide for "greenhorns" like us. He and six other fellows made up our fishing expedition. We learned that the others in our group were not any more "expert" in this business than we were.

All of us went by car to our rendezvous in the Oregon mountains and met on a plain perhaps sixty-five miles south of Portland. Jim had thought of everything. Each of us had a saddle horse. We also had a tent large enough to sleep eight or ten men in sleeping bags, all our food, and everything else we would need for our expedition. The packhorse was a big mule. Tom's horse was an Indian pony, and my mount was *supposed* to be gentle. Jim led off, and we followed single file up the mountain. This was June, and in valleys we found deep snow, often up to the belly of our horses. We climbed quickly to get to a high mountain lake by a sloping hillside for our camp. We got the big tent up with places for sleeping bags on the lakeshore. What sheer magnificent beauty all around us. Tired as we were, Jim cooked a big supper and we ate.

Jim, Tom, and I slept under a big tent, with the lake in front of us, the stars above, the horses nearby, munching food and switching flies with their tails, and dreaming of tomorrow.

One day Tom and I stood on the sandy shore of the big lake to fish. When we got a "keeper" we just tossed it behind us in the huge snow bank and kept it cold until we were ready to clean and cook. It was great.

Jim gave us a good breakfast of bacon, eggs, and all else that was needed.

Tom was adventurous. He rode his Indian pony bareback and raced around the camp like a wild man! Jim had a large inner tube we used as a float on the lake. That was okay for Tom but not for me!

I was walking around the lake, casting now and then, and looked across the lake and saw a big trout lying in about four feet of water, under a log. I got Tom's attention and he came over. I showed him the big fish. He put on the correct lure, cast just above the trout, let the lure slowly sink, gave it a couple of twitches and WOW! what a fish! He fought all the way. I was so proud of the way Tom handled the fish. The other men saw the action and ran over to the water. It was a fourteen-inch rainbow trout—delicious when cooked over Jim's open fire.

One day Jim decided we should ride across the mountain. Part of the way we walked and led our horses single file. It was quite risky but fun.

The last day we got up early, took down the tent, and fixed all baggage for the packhorse. Jim led to break path through deep snow banks. Tom and I also had to lead the packhorse, which got tired and laid down. We got Jim to come back to get the mule up and all went okay. It was a great time for Tom and me.

We got back to family camp and my dear wife and Sue. We all had a wonderful three days, camping and eating burned "stuff" cooked camp style! What a wonderful experience. From there we went south to the leader's camp at Santa Rosa, California, and then on home.

Another Western Assignment

As secretary of the Board of Christian Education, I was serving the smallest of national agencies. That means I was the lowest paid executive, I had the smallest travel budget. I was expected to serve as recording secretary for many things (always without extra pay).

I was responsible for my own travel arrangements. When Tom and Sue were small I always tried to drive and the whole family went together. Gertie, Tom, and Sue have had to suffer through countless conventions and camp meetings and often lived in less than luxurious accommodations. Here is how it happened one summer. I was to be speaker for both the Washington and Oregon camp meetings with five or six days in between the two.

Ray Bringham was pastor in western Colorado and in charge of a small "western slope" camp meeting. He would guarantee one hundred dollars if I would be their evangelist, stopping there on our return trip. I accepted. We did a lot of sight seeing on our way west— Iowa, the Badlands of South Dakota, the Sioux Indian reservation in South Dakota, Yellowstone Park, Wyoming, Montana, Glacier National Park, Columbia River Gorge, Seattle, Portland, Inland Empire Camp Meeting, the magnificent drive south on Oregon's coastal route to the Redwood areas, Big Sur Country, and back over the mountains to Colorado's western slope camp meeting. What a marvelous summer with many educational opportunities.

We got to Colorado with directions to the Church of God campground. I had only a few dollars left and these were pre-credit card days. We got some hamburgers and gasoline and continued our quest.

At last we found it. The Church of God camp grounds! We saw a tabernacle and counted eleven people singing "Heavenly Sunlight" like a funeral dirge. Obviously not the Church of God grounds we wanted. Tom was about twelve years old. Sue was eight. Tom climbed back into our car and said, "Dad, if that is really ours, I fear for the movement." We all did. We drove on and finally found our destination; they were singing as lively as Herb Thompson ever did and Ray Bringham came out to greet us. I was wearing my old scratched leather jacket (a Christmas gift from Gertie and Tom—five years earlier) and sport shirt. No matter—they were ready for my sermon. What sermon? But I preached, God blessed, and the camp meeting was on!

Ray was a tall blond with wavy hair, a wide smile, and infectious enthusiasm—an outgoing friendly blond bear. Paul and Thelma Whalen were in charge of music. We already knew them and many other people, so it was a fun time, and the Lord blessed to our good and his glory. Years later Ray was director of the National Prayer Summit. I need to pray more. I am too practical.

On this trip we stood on the Great Divide at the entrance to the vast panorama before us, with a basin hundreds of miles across and majestic mountain ranges (the Grand Tetons) marching across the horizon. Tom said, "Dad, if I could see this once a year I could endure anything." We all felt it; Tom said it.

The office of this new agency where I was now employed was quite small. Located in the Warner Press building, it was formerly a storage closet, about ten feet wide and twenty feet long. The windows opened to the tar-covered roof of the Warner Press printing area. There were three desks, two old typewriters, and an old dictating machine—all borrowed from other agencies. It was simple to make fund deposits or withdrawals; there were small slips of paper near a "cash box" or a desk drawer. Slips were marked IN or OUT and used accordingly. This was my new office. Betty Jo Hutchison and Thelma Whalen ran the office, such as it was. From these women I got my orientation in the work of the Board of Christian Education.

The board members were elected by the General Assembly and usually served terms of three years. There was a board of directors of five members. The former executive secretary, Irene Smith Caldwell, was still a member of the Board. Irene Caldwell was the Board's first full time administrator. She had married Mack Caldwell a few months prior to my coming. For the interim the board had selected R. Eugene Sterner to serve as chief executive.

One important lesson I learned had to do with the *Standard Leadership Curriculum*. This was a most interesting program, crafted by representatives of some thirty plus Protestant church boards of Christian education, administered during this time by the International Council of Religious Education (ICRE) and the separate denominational boards of Christian education.

The curriculum was designed to provide basic study courses for church school teachers and leaders. It provided courses on four levels of study. First series courses required study of an approved text and a minimum of five hours in classes in-group study. Second series courses were twice as intensive, and third series more advanced. I think the fourth series courses were never fully developed.

Each series (or level of study) was designed to cover such basic courses as these: Personal Religious Living, Bible (both Old and New Testament), Understanding Persons and How They Learn, Methods of Teaching Developed by Age Groups. A few illustrations will help to make this clear:

110a Personal Religious Living
110b Personal Religious Living
210a Understanding How Persons Learn

After the general courses there were age group studies, e.g. pre-school, kindergarten, beginners, primaries, juniors, junior high, and so forth. Similar, teaching method courses went from the general to more specific, such as Story Telling, How to Lead a Discussion, and so forth. In the same manner Bible courses became particularized (Life and Teachings of Jesus, Life and Ministry of Paul, the Gospels, Psalms, Acts of the Apostles, and so on). Special or specific courses could be added by a denominational board; for example, Church History could be particularized to include such a course as "The Origin and Early Days of the Church of God (or Methodist or Presbyterian Church).

For each course satisfactorily completed, a student received a three-by-five-inch certificate of course completion. Five such cards made one eligible for the First Certificate of Progress, and so on, through ten, twenty, and thirty hours of study, leading eventually to a handsome Certificate of Achievement. Credits earned inter-denominationally were transferable to one's own church record. Each year I signed and awarded thousands of credits and many Certificates of Progress.

Many local communities offered courses in community "schools" at least twice a year. Some larger churches offered their own schools, usually lasting eight to ten weeks, with a large number of courses, often with guest leaders for particular courses. In Detroit, Michigan, the Metropolitan Church of God would offer a wide range of studies and special "graduation" events in autumn and spring. I was outside speaker for many of these graduation events.

While we recognize many weaknesses in these schools, we must also praise honest efforts to equip teachers and leaders with at least basic studies and thousands benefited by these efforts. *The Standard Leadership Development Curriculum* was not a small thing and the smaller church groups especially suffered immeasurable losses when the program was officially discontinued.

Along with the Board of Christian Education, other general agencies had their offices in the Gospel Trumpet Company building (World Service, the Missionary Board, the Board of Pensions, and the Women of the Church of God). One day each of us found on his desk a memo from Dr. A. T. Rowe, General Manager of Gospel Trumpet Company, stating that we could no longer house our offices in their building. We had to make other arrangements. The World Service Office did some remodeling in what is now Byrum Hall, and the Board of Christian Education rented one apartment in a building located on the corner of Fifth Street and College Drive. These and others were all temporary arrangements.

Meantime Clarence Hatch, Lawrence Brooks, A. W. Miller, a representative of the women's board, and I began conversations eventually leading to a new building we planned to erect, which we called the Missions Building. I was named treasurer and

Ground Breaking Missions Building

manager. It took a lot of planning and careful study, but we did finally erect our own building.

My day by day work in Christian education called for lots of correspondence. By this time I was convinced that we needed to give attention to developing state boards of Christian education. Only a few states gave any help for their people through a state board or committee on Christian education. I gave a lot of energy to helping states set up such an organization. It was also work and meant lots of travel, but slowly I was successful.

When I became secretary of the Board of Christian Education, I had little formal training in that field. Harold Phillips and Carl Kardatzke encouraged me to enroll at Butler University School of Religion. The next few years were extremely difficult, but I did complete the seminary work for an advanced degree. I was also writing Sunday school curriculum materials for Lottie Franklin; this I did for weeks at a time, starting about 9:30 at night and working on it for about two hours, writing again from five to six o'clock in the morning, before leaving at 6:45 A.M. for class in Indianapolis. Afternoons, early evenings, and most weekends, were spent at the office, or preaching, or leading a conference somewhere. I guess anyone can do what one really wants to do—when the belief is strong enough.

Campaigns such as the United Church School Advance (1962) and the Mid-century Evangelistic Advance (1959) all kept evangelism alive and vital. I had the honor of serving on these and other similar committees and was the chairman and administrator of both these and others in the Church of God.

A careful study of church growth was made at Louisville Kentucky Seminary. It examined the usual and commonly accepted courses of church growth, but found no one item could be thought of as directly influencing growth—not location, not the pastor, not the time of preaching, not eloquent preaching, not the time of worship service— none of these. They did find a direct and causal relationship between the number of effectively functioning church groups and church growth. This included Sunday school classes, Bible study classes, men's and women's youth groups, scout troops, fellowship groups, choirs, and so on.

Following this study many of us in Christian education turned our attention to focus on group life in the church. At the same time the study of the dynamics of group life came under careful scrutiny nationally. I had already learned something about the Oxford Group Movement, when as an Anderson College student, I was helped by Dr. Wesley Bransford, pastor of Anderson's First Methodist Church. In the next months we held many conferences exploring group dynamics in the church. We began to see successful group life as essential to evangelism. We encouraged the formation of *Vocational Koinonia,* VK Groups. A VK group is a gathering of school teachers, secretaries, directors or professors—all in a similar vocation—who could turn that group into a center of redemptive love—Koinonia. We were beginning to see that, indeed, the journey is our home.

My first calling in ministry was in evangelism. In those early days most congregations of the Church of God planned on having at least two revival meetings with a visiting evangelist every year. It was in that kind of setting that my ministry began. For many years I had frequent calls for evangelistic preaching, and I tried to combine with preaching a strong emphasis on the role of teachers in nurture and discipleship.

I have vivid memories of the ministry of such preachers as Ross Minkler, J. W. Lykins, J. Lee Collins, W. F. Chappel, W. F. Coy, E. E. Wolfram, Lawrence Hatch, H. M. Riggle, and C. H. Featherston. Some of these concentrated their preaching in basic doctrines of the Church of God, but all preached with passion and fervor. Some of them had a strong influence on my own journey of faith.

Evangelism was always part of the journey. There was strong emphasis on mass meetings, later strongly influenced by the dynamic new evangelist Billy Graham.

Literature evangelism also began very early in this movement. *The Gospel Trumpet* (later to become *Vital Christianity*), pamphlets, tracts, and other papers were tools for evangelism. When I made my first trip from Cedar Rapids, Iowa, to Anderson, Indiana, to attend the annual camp meeting, I was twelve years old. Three of us sat in the rear seat of Pastor Swecker's open touring Ford. On country roads as we came to a farmer's mailbox, we would toss out a copy or two of *The Gospel Trumpet* (literature evangelism)!

Those were the days of many *new* ventures: helping hundreds of churches organize a board of Christian education or a church council; helping about forty states and districts organize their educational work; planning and conducting scores of Sunday school conventions and youth conventions; starting and administering National Leaders' Camps and Laboratory Training Schools; organizing and administering the Christian Volunteer Training Schools, forerunner of the Tri-S program at Anderson University; starting and directing world work camps, world conferences, and bringing the national youth work into a full department of the board's responsibilities.

Director, Board of Christian Education
Miller, Haldeman, Kardatske, Franklin, Phillips

International Youth Convention

Early in my tenure we agreed to absorb the "independent" youth convention and let it be a part of our youth department. That also had far reaching influence in our total program.

I was about sixteen years old when I attended my first youth convention. A year later, at Ottumwa, Iowa, I was elected president; I had so much to learn! Now, many years later, in 1948 in Denver, Colorado, I had become the treasurer of the International Youth Convention.

It is our custom to have a state (or area) youth convention every year. Many of these are held on Thanksgiving weekend. In years following, I was the guest speaker twice for these conventions: I was the speaker at the eighteenth in Miami, Florida (1952), and at the twenty-first in Philadelphia, Pennsylvania (1958).

There would be one or more featured speakers and probably some group of musicians. Many important decisions by many young people have been made in these meetings. Also many young people from smaller churches get an expanding view of the church as they mingle with so many other Christian young persons.

Important as these state meetings are, they cannot take the place of the larger international youth conventions. Our international youth convention is held every other year in the summer months. In the early days the meeting was held on a college campus or in a large hotel. Who can count the life changing decisions made at youth conventions in South Bend, Milwaukee, St. Louis, Los Angeles, Washington DC, Atlanta, Denver, Portland, Toronto, Edmonton, Houston, Philadelphia, or other places? Today, IYC takes place in convention centers and huge convention halls, but its purpose and effectiveness remain the same. Thank God for these great meetings and the people whose leadership makes them possible.

Smile A While

When our son, Tom, and his fiancée, Sandra, were to be married, they asked me to read the ceremony. I was honored and quickly accepted. The wedding was to be held in the beautiful sanctuary of the Park Place Church of God in Anderson, Indiana. A large crowd had gathered for the event. The ceremony had been carefully rehearsed. The music began and was played to perfection. I began reading the ceremony. When the bride and groom knelt for prayer, I heard some muffled laughter and it bothered me; briefly I wondered what I had said that was inappropriate, but I kept on with the prayer. The laughter became more noticeable. When I said the "Amen," I looked up and most of the people were laughing, trying hard not to show it. I could hardly believe it. Only much later, after the reception, did I learn what had happened. Before the ceremony began, Tom's best man had taken Tom's shoes and printed on one shoe in bold white ink the letters **H E** *and on the other shoe the letters* **L P.** *When Tom and Sandy knelt for prayer, of course, everyone in the audience read that silent plea for assistance. They all laughed, but neither Gertie nor I thought it was funny. I confess that both of us found it difficult to have a forgiving attitude toward the wedding attendant who did that, but Tom never did show how he really felt about it. Some people thought it was funny, I didn't. How would you feel?*

Colorado Fishing

In the year of the youth convention in Portland, Oregon, Tom Smith, my son Tom, and I drove together as far as Denver, Colorado. Tom Smith left us there and flew on to Portland. He was in charge of the convention and needed some extra days there for advance preparation. My son Tom and I drove from the Denver airport to a ranch near the Grand Teton National Park. We had made reservations for a cabin on the ranch. It was rustic but comfortable and adequate to our needs. We spent a few days exploring and fishing in rivers and streams. We did not catch many trout and were feeling down hearted, when the owner of the ranch told us of a place where he was certain we could get some trout.

We followed the man's directions to a hill overlooking a valley that was the head waters of a river. This was the summer feeding grounds for some moose! We parked the car and climbed down a home-made rope ladder to the base of a high bluff. Getting to the lake about which we had been told was challenging, for we had to avoid deep holes the moose had made in their wanderings. Our friend, Mr. Gunderson, the ranch owner, had described the "canoe" he had made and we found it easily. It was all aluminum and steel, and was made from the gasoline tank from an airplane. Our host had assured us it was safe and adequate to our needs. We put our fishing tackle and what personal things we had in the canoe and cast off. We got about twenty feet from shore and discovered our load was too heavy; the canoe was not leaking but was taking in water, and soon sank, with Tom and me standing in it! The water was not deep, and in some way we managed to get out of the sunken boat, retrieve our fishing tackle, and wade to shore, pulling the canoe after us. We were two very wet, very muddy, very frightened fishermen! We did not return to the car immediately, but tried fishing from the bank in a few different places. No fish today! We finally got back to the rope ladder and climbed to the top of the bluff to where our car was. I now recall that Tom said, "Dad—you know if I did this without you, when you discovered it you would severely reprimand me, wouldn't you?" I had to agree. In our climbing around, in and out of the tracks of moose, we often got on the tops of large clumps covered with branches and sticks, and which we later learned were beaver houses! We could so easily have fallen through, and given an unwelcome visit to a family of angry beavers! Any way, we scraped off some of the mud, got into our car, and drove back to our cabin. We removed all our muddy clothes, which had absorbed much of the unpleasant aroma of the swamp, got showered, into clean clothes, and drove to the nearest restaurant, about fifteen miles away. We had to discard most of our clothing, so we bought new clothes the next day and drove toward Yellowstone National Park. We were able to get good lodging just outside the park. The following day we did some guided fishing for cut-throat trout. Tom did not catch anything, but I did, and we had it prepared for a delicious dinner. We fished again the next day, and this time it was Tom who brought in a large cut-throat trout, which was our evening dinner.

World Conference

The Board of Christian Education sponsored the bi-annual international Youth Convention. Tom A. Smith, as the national director of youth work, had responsibility for planning and administering the youth convention. I was treasurer. Dondeena Fleenor Caldwell was president. When we met in Miami, Florida, a visitor at the convention was an Anderson College student from Zurich, Switzerland, Esther Waurich. The president asked her to bring greetings from the young people of Europe. She said, "You call this an *international convention,* yet it includes only Canada and the United States. We invite your convention to Europe and you could become truly international." The audience gave a resounding response of cheers.

Later Tom and I discussed the possibility of taking the convention to Europe. We had a small Bible College in Fritzlar, Germany, of which Dr. Ernst Kersten was president; we thought we should consult with them, maybe they would host such a meeting. We talked further with our own leaders, and we received from Dr. Kersten an invitation to hold our convention in Fritzlar in the summer of 1955.

Russell Olt, dean of Anderson College, and Adam Miller, executive of the Church of God Missionary Board, had in partnership a modest travel agency. Both men had visited Fritzlar and knew the German Church of God quite well. We invited them to prepare for us a low-cost tour of Central Europe culminating with a youth convention in Fritzlar. This they did. It would be based on steamship travel from New York City to England, medium priced hotels, two meals a day, land travel by a chartered bus, and/or by second class coach train travel, sightseeing at many appropriate places. They proposed such a tour and we began advertising. To get moral support, able speakers, and church agency financial underwriting we proposed that persons such as J. A. Morrison, Robert Reardon, C. W. Hatch, Mrs. Ocie Perry, and Dale Oldham be used as program leaders. Most of the Anderson based agencies agreed (some reluctantly) to participate in financial underwriting.

An enormous amount of correspondence by mail and many long-distance phone calls used much of our energies in the weeks that followed. It was not long until eighty-four people had signed up for the tour. For travel purposes we made four teams of twenty each, with Tom Smith, Dean Olt, A. W. Miller, and I each responsible for a group. Elmer Kardatzke, pastor of the Church of God

World Conference Planning Meeting, Nairobi, Kenya

in Wichita, Kansas, made his own arrangements to lead a group of about twenty persons, flying Trans-Atlantic. Many others negotiated their own arrangements, coming singly or in small groups. The larger group of more than eighty persons went by ship (The M.S. Italia)

On board M.S. Italia bound for Germany

from New York City to England. Using professional tour guides, we did sight seeing before and after the convention in England, Scotland, France, Belgium, Holland, Luxembourg, Switzerland, Germany, Austria, Italy, and Lichtenstein. Most of us had no previous experience in European travel; all of us made the most of our new situations. Students from the Bible school met us at the main station in Fritzlar with harmonizing singing of songs and hymns.

Our meetings were held in the low ceiling town hall, in the Bible school, and in the Fritzlar Church of God. There were delegates from Germany, France, Italy, Holland, England, Denmark, Canada, the United States, Lebanon, Cypress, Egypt, Kenya, Tanzania, Barbados, Trinidad, Greece, Mexico, India, Japan, Jamaica, Brazil, and Argentina. We did not all speak the same language, but all of us felt and understood and used the language of Christian love! It was truly a humbling and an exhilarating experience. The Holy Spirit was in control, making one body out of many persons with very different customs and backgrounds. Our low horizons and limited visions were fast expanding in this indivisible fellowship of believers.

For many of us memories of World War II were still vivid as we recalled traumatic moments of that horrible war. In one city which had been heavily bombed in the war, men and women sat in the rubble patiently cleaning bricks for use in rebuilding. One man in our group, an American Air Force veteran, openly wept as he saw the unspeakable damage done by bombs that perhaps he had dropped. There was unabashed confession of guilt both personal and national, seeking forgiveness and healing and forging of new bonds of Christian fellowship. God helped us to redefine boundaries of Christian witness as the Holy Spirit probed our ambitions, our relationships, our goals and procedures.

Our mass meetings and smaller cluster groups studied the Bible trying to sense its relevance to this time and place; there were serious moments of recommitment of our dreams and our energies. This was for all of us a crucial turning point and defining week of truth. We sang, prayed, laughed, wept, confessed, joined hands and hearts in a new fellowship!

2nd World Conference, 1929 Essen, Germany

Those of us who came back to New York on the M.S. Italia gathered each day to continue our fellowship, to reflect on our personal and corporate experience, and to seek God's guidance as we planned for the future. We found that all of us were thinking we surely must plan for another "truly international" experience. We all came to the conviction that four years hence we should have another such convention, and this time we should accept the invitation to the church in Essen, Germany. We set in motion plans for such a meeting and I was asked to be responsible for making it happen. I did! We had already been referring to the Fitzlar meeting as a world conference, so now we freely used that term not to replace the usual international youth convention, but have it in the even numbered years, meeting bi-annually, and the world conference meeting every four years. I was the director and treasurer for the next three world conferences: Essen, Germany, in 1959; Bochum, Germany, in 1963; and Zurich, Switzerland, in 1967.

Each convention was unique. We had many new delegates and new challenges and opportunities; as the world was changing, so was the church changing.

In the Essen Convention our host was Gerhart Klabunde, director of the printing company for the German Church of God. To identify him further, his younger daughter Edith later was married to Rev. Willi Krenz, and his son, Herbert Klabunde became the husband of Hyla Quinn, a strong and effective lay church leader in her own right. The Essen Convention began with mass meetings on Sunday and closed the following Sunday afternoon with another mass meeting. Also all registered delegates were asked to stay in the big convention hotel. This was not easy. German pastors who lived near Essen found it difficult to understand why they should stay in a hotel. We patiently explained the need for cohesiveness in the convention and the need for all of us to become better acquainted with each other; reluctantly most of them were cooperative with us. Women of the Essen Church had carefully made beautiful flags to be carried by designated representatives of each nation represented in the convention. The opening and later closing sessions featured a procession of national delegates led by the designated flag-bearer. It was stirring, colorful, sobering, and challenging.

Each convention program was planned to explore and develop a theme based on scripture and unique to that specific meeting. After each convention we used a variety of procedures to obtain delegate evaluations. Although each convention was quite expensive, I was able to return significant amounts to agency underwriters.

All opening and closing sessions of the Bochum Convention in 1963 were held in a large Protestant church we had rented for the occasion. Each week night leased buses helped us move to another city and church for the evening meeting. A different local church was host for each evening event. All the public services had a strong evangelistic emphasis.

By the time of the Zurich Convention I had persuaded the Executive Council it was really their responsibility to direct the World Conference, as opposed to having the Board of Christian Education carry the total adminis- trative load and the inherent financial risks. I served as a consultant for Zurich and later for the convention in Oaxtepec, Mexico. A convention had been planned for Beirut, Lebanon, for 1971, but was canceled because of the war in Lebanon.

T. Franklin Miller and Gertie honored at World Conference, Birmingham, England

Tom Smith was a colleague and ally in many of these ventures. I gladly gave support to Tom in bringing great world leaders to the international youth conventions. Many Church of God young people were exposed to and enriched by the great wisdom and insight of Dr. Kagawa, Dr. E. Stanley Jones, Dr. Samuel Moffatt, and others. The international youth conventions could never have been so successful without the help and participation of many other Church of God leaders, such as Walter Haldeman, A.T. and Ida Byrd Rowe, Gene Newberry, Harold Phillips, Dale Oldham, Kenneth Hall, Lottie Franklin, Edith Lindenman, Arlene Stevens (Hall), Paul and Thelma Whalen, Betty Jo Hutchison, Bessie Willowby, John and Margaret Smith, Clara Lorton (Smith), Bob and Dorothy Nicholson, Mildred Hatch, Esther Bauer, Wilma Hale, Robert Reardon, Arlo Newell, Kenneth Prunty, Donald Courtney, and Sherrill Hayes. This is a long and incomplete list of close colleagues, helpers, mentors, asso- ciates, and loyal friends. God bless them all!

Smile A While

When my friend Lee Lewis was a pastor, I was preaching on Sunday morning at the conclusion of an intensive week of evangelistic preaching. We were standing and singing the second stanza of the hymn of invitation when I heard muffled snickers and then laughter. Hazel Lewis, wife of the pastor, was sitting in the second pew, just behind a whole row of teenage boys, a sort of gang led by one they called Mack. Hazel had just seen Mack get all of his boys in a huddle, and heard him say, "Okay, gang, it's time to get going, so move it now!" And they all went like one person to kneel at the prayer altar. No wonder Hazel laughed.

Evangelism and Nurture

When our son Tommy was about three years old, I came into the living room at home and found him trying to push a table across the floor. "Son," I said, "You can't do that! The table is as big as your are." Without slowing his efforts he quickly responded, "I can, too. I am as big as the table." It doesn't change the size of the table, but the way we look at it changes our ability to move the table. So in this calling to proclaim and to nurture, we say with the Apostle Paul, "I can do all things through Christ who strengthens me." We are as big as the table!

In those days as the chief executive of our national Board of Christian Education, I often said that proclamation and nurture are twins. Evangelism and Christian teaching, at their best, need each other.

I kept telling people that a bird was made to fly and it needs two wings. With only one wing a bird can hop and jump and run, but it cannot fly. It needs two wings. So do we. We must have excellence in both evangelism and its twin, Christian nurture. An Indian Bishop of the Methodist Church said evangelism is one beggar telling another beggar where he found bread. We who have found bread must tell others how and where we found it. Our calling is to confront persons with the living Christ and call for a decision—a total commitment. All teaching must be in the light of the cross, either anticipating it and seeking its healing message or, seeing its shadow, we are looking back to see how to live in the light of the cross of Christ. Teaching must call for a decision: "What will you do with Jesus, the Christ of God?"

My first calling in ministry was in evangelism. In these early days most congregations of the Church of God planned on having at least two revival meetings with an outside evangelist every year. It was in that setting I began my preaching ministry. I still believe in "preaching for a verdict." Until recent months, I had frequent calls for evangelistic preaching. This ministry has taken me to all parts of the USA, and the Lord has blessed with great success, especially in reaching young people and young adults.

Many years later, when I was president of Warner Press, we supplemented these efforts by subsidizing thousands of books and tens of thousands of other items. One such effort included a printing of 10,000 copies of *This We Believe, This We Proclaim* by Earl Martin. It was distributed through local churches in lots of one hundred copies at wholesale printing costs. Literature evangelism!

There were other efforts in outreach. Periodically we had an evangelistic emphasis, such as special subscription prices for *The Gospel Trumpet.* The advent of radio broadcasting and television preaching made a new way for evangelism. The Sunday school became a means of evangelism and outreach. Special campaigns brought new enthusiasm to Sunday school workers after tying in with a popular slogan or plan to boost enrollment and reach new people. One plan, in 1933–34, called for the starting of 1000 new Sunday schools. More than six hundred were thus started. Also in the early days of the "flying ministry" street preaching and the formation of evangelistic companies (often only four or five members) were tools of outreach. The message was also published in several different languages, notably German and Scandinavian. Bible training schools were set up to train volunteer "missionaries" for visitation and evangelism so that at one time there were more than forty such missionary homes. There were special campaigns such as one conducted by the International Council of Religious Education over a four year period: "Find Them, Reach Them, Win Them, Train Them," with lots of supportive material. Through some effort we became connected to "neighborhood evangelism" and evangelism became popularized and utilized. We were using many different approaches that by many ways we might win some. Evangelism for many decades was at the very heart and center of the Church of God movement.

In the midst of those busy years, Dr. Morrison surprised me by asking me to become dean of the School of Theology. Along with other general agency leaders, I had helped get the "SOT" started and had taught many Christian education classes there. I thanked Dr. Morrison for his confidence, but I refused the position because I knew I was not qualified for it academically, nor in other ways.

I stayed put and continued with the Board of Christian Education for several more years. The nature of the position required representation on several other boards and committees, such as World Service and the Executive Council. I often ended up serving as recording secretary for these committees, and my dear friend and faithful servant of the Lord, Edith Lindenman, typed what I recorded—literally *thousands* of pages of minutes and records. I could never convey enough gratitude to Edith! Those were the days of national campaigns in the church: the Quarter Million Campaign, the Mid-century Evangelistic Advance, the Diamond Jubilee, and the Centennial Celebration. In addition to my main responsibilities with the Board of Christian Education, I often helped in directing these national campaigns. The years during which the national Board of Christian Education was growing were certainly never dull ones!

Mid-century Evangelistic Advance

In the early 1940s we began talking about an appropriate church celebration of 1950—the mid-century mark. Charles Weber had been given several suggestions, all of which centered on evangelism. So we agreed on a Mid-century Evangelistic Advance and began planning for it.

In those days the most popular presentations included flip charts, and filmstrips (with accompanying sound and motion pictures). For help we turned to our friends at the Detroit based Jam Handy Corporation (named for the founder and owner, Mr. Jamison Handy). They had made a vast number of training films for the United States military. It was agreed that I should take a one-day trip to Detroit and present our needs to the people at Jam Handy, such as Scott Mitchell and Russell McCracken. Sue, our daughter, was about five-years-old, so I arranged for her to fly with me. There were not many on our flight, so the stewardess asked her to assist. (I think she distributed napkins and maybe peanuts.) She had a good time. Scott Mitchell of Mr. Handy's staff was to meet us at the airport, but he had car trouble and was late. It was almost noon when he arrived, so he took Sue and me to lunch. He asked Sue what she wanted and she asked for a steak. Scott asked how she wanted it cooked and she said, "Just like daddy has his!" So we all had steak—delicious! Later I made my presentation to Scott's colleagues. Still later Sue and I got on the plane for our return home.

In due time we completed plans for observing the "mid-century." In the local church this included flip charts on personal evangelism, materials for revival meetings and special evangelistic efforts, and finally our agreement to make a motion picture appropriate to the theme. We also made room for fund-raising, cooperatively, with each national agency a chance to promote a special project. The ultimate goal was a million dollars extra—to be raised among *men* of the church. We organized carefully for this.

We invited about one hundred to one hundred fifty men to many regional meetings for a dinner at a hotel on a Friday evening. Everett Hartung was the national chairperson and we employed Lester Crose to set-up the meetings and follow through. After dinner Dale Oldham gave a motivational talk, asking each man for cash or a pledge for at least one thousand dollars. Some gave generously up to $50,000. When Dale could not take the service, I was next in line, and I took many of these meetings. We offered each agency the names, addresses, and pledge information of every man present. So far as I could learn, Anderson College was the only one that carefully followed the campaign. They did a *good* job of it and raised a lot of money. When I inquired of the donors about their pledge, I got the same answer over and over again—"Nobody ever before asked me for that much money"! We raised a lot of money over and above the World Service giving.

The third major ingredient of the Mid-century Evangelistic Advance was the motion picture. This we debated at great length. Finally Jam Handy sent Russell McCracken, professional film producer, and he spent a few days with us, asking, listening, and learning. He was with Harold Phillips for several hours. He left with a car full of books about the Church of God. When he later returned he brought a script. We gathered with great interest as he read *From Heaven to Earth*. Dr. Nicholson was our advisor and decision-maker on the music—that was skillfully done.

After the script was read we discussed it at length. Dr. Morrison spoke first, expressing disappointment that so little was said about the general agencies. We debated. Finally McCracken emphasized that he was depicting people caught up in a golden dream, a spirit of gentle humility and courage, a devotion to an ideal, captivated by a compelling and loving vision. We decided on a black and white film. We prepared suggestions for showing it in a local church or a large gathering in a community and various other showings. We agreed on a price per copy for sale and rental fee, with Warner Press handling distribution.

This movie was a major effort and that we reached agreement on so many issues is a salute to our cooperative endeavor in the Mid-century Evangelistic Advance. Charles Weber, who had been serving as chairperson of the campaign, felt he could no longer continue in that role and resigned at the end of three of his five years. I was asked to carry that responsibility to the conclusion. It was indeed a mighty effort calling for a great investment of energy and fine leadership.

VIII

Neighbors in Anderson

On a cold late October morning in Anderson, I met Dr. A. T. Rowe, president of the Gospel Trumpet company, to dig and transplant trees! A nursery was cleaning out much of its stock at one dollar an item (tree or shrub), but we had to take everything as we went. Dr. Rowe was wearing knee-high rubber boots, jeans, and heavy shirt and sweater. I was dressed warmly; both of us ready for outside work. I had told Dr. Rowe that although we had just recently taken steps to purchase lots for a new house we planned to build, we had no idea where to plant trees or what kind to plant. It made no difference to him. So we dug trees. Company trucks came to haul them to their new homes. Some that we transplanted, oak and elm trees, all still growing. Just six years ago I helped to cut down an elm tree that Dr. Rowe and I had planted so long ago!

There were not many people living in the area where we planted trees. Most of that land had been a part of the orchard of the Gospel Trumpet Company communal farm, and was now being sold as residential building sites. A new neighborhood was in the making.

Tom Dearing, owner of Dearing's East Side Drug Store, lived in an attractive house on the southeast corner of East Seventh and Chestnut Street. Just two houses north, on Chestnut, was where Wilbur and Eileen Shield lived with a ground level garage built into the hillside. We planted an elm tree on the rear of that small lot. In later years the Dearing house was owned by Dr. and Mrs. James Earl Massey. Tom Ramsey got Russell Byrum to construct a house, and we built on the lots just east at 1210 East Seventh Street. We planted a

white birch tree in what would have been our backyard, but it lived only a few years.

Across the street from our house was a huge gravel pit. When Russell Byrum was building our house he said there was a very thick vein of pure sand going south into the gravel pit. When Bill Bowser built his house across the street from us, they hauled in many loads of fill dirt and years later paid for it when the sewer line broke and the porous concrete blocks of the wall absorbed much of the drainage and major repairs became necessary.

One night a couple of years later we had a knock on the front door. Edith Ramsey was there, frantically calling for help. It was raining very hard. I put on a raincoat and ran next door, west, where the Ramsey's had recently moved to a new house. They needed help! Furniture had been moved into the living room and the dining floor had two or three inches of water! What a comedy of errors. Tom Ramsey was on hands and knees with an electric drill boring holes in the floor. I asked "Why," he replied testily to "drain the water, couldn't you see?" Water was everywhere. A neighbor woman was scooping up water in a pail, poured it down the kitchen sink, and it promptly came out the toilet in the bathroom. What a mess—funny but crazy! Tom had called Russell Byrum builder of the house, who stood patiently in the living room water, and kept asking Ramsey if he wanted Russell to dig down to the sewer in the front yard. Tom almost lost his religion as he screamed, "Well, for heaven's sake, do something!" Russell made no reply, but in a few minutes he and some of his men were digging in the mud in the front yard. I could not avoid laughing! They broke a tile and found wedged in it a small piece of two-by-four, causing all that damage. Later I tried to tease Tom about trying to drain the water in small drill holes. He did not see anything funny about it. Not a good sense of humor.

To some of our present neighbors and to many of our former neighbors, I offer a sincere apology. Two of the trees Dr. Rowe and I planted were not oak or maple, but cottonwood. We planted several. I remember only two, because they are still living, but I do not know why we planted them where they are. At a certain time of the year, the cottonwood tree fills the entire neighborhood with fine cotton that intuitively seeks, finds, and adheres to any door or window screen.

These trees we planted do live up to their reputation. The two I remember were planted next door to property owned by Opal Bengtson, now owned by Dan and Betty Harman. The two trees are very tall and very prolific. I heard that Dan paid someone one hundred dollars to cut down the trees, but the agent removed only the lowest (under fifty feet) branches, leaving the ugly top. So, good neighbors, I apologize. We should have planted oak trees and reserved these two "cotton factories" for a public park!

To Gene and Agnes Newberry, Gertie and I owe a debt of gratitude. Our guest book dates back to the days of the Federal Housing Authority (FHA), a government agency that in the 1940s made possible low-interest loans for residential construction. The FHA required a certain percentage of wages in income to secure the loans. Gene had finally qualified when a small nearby Presbyterian church engaged him to preach for them every Sunday for three months and assured him of fifteen dollars a week. That guarantee put the Newberry income just slightly above the floor needed to get their FHA loan for a new home. When that was approved, Gene told me and I applied for a grant with a similar preaching assignment for a few months following the Newberry tenure. That amount was just enough to put the Miller loan application slightly above minimum requirement, so we got our FHA loan and proceeded to have Russell Byrum construct our house. I have never learned how much political "pull" was involved in that transaction, but neither has anyone (so far as I know) ever inquired about either Gertie's or my political persuasion.

Smile A While

When Bessie Brown Willowby was employed as a field worker for the Board of Christian Education, one Sunday morning for her opening appearance in a certain church she sang a solo. As she returned to her seat, she tripped on a loose carpet and fell flat on her face. The song she had just sung was, "Open My Eyes That I May See." Bessie laughed as she told this story on herself. I think I know how she felt, regardless of how badly her body was bruised.

The Board of Christian Education had given approval to employing field workers; usually we could not afford more than one at a time. One of our first such was Bessie Brown, a recent graduate of Anderson College with a major in Christian education. She would typically spend a week with a church, starting Saturday and going through Friday. This was not easy work, but Bessie did it well and was well received.

I did most of the scheduling for Bessie's itinerary and we kept her busy. One day she confided in me that she had met a handsome and interesting man, and he would like to see her again. When I could, I rearranged her schedule so she could see more of John Willowby. The romance grew and eventually Bessie and John became engaged. The wedding was set for a summer weekend. Bessie asked Gertie to sing at the wedding; she also used Tom and Sue; and I officiated. It was a beautiful wedding.

Bessie and John stayed on in Kansas, always busy as lay persons in the church. We visited them in their home more than once. Bessie became chairperson of the Kansas Board of Christian Education and kept a place in the national work at the same time. They were on a mission of teaching in Oklahoma, after driving all night, when they fell asleep at the wheel, crossed the highway median-strip, hit an oncoming semi truck, and were killed almost instantly. It was a great loss to the church.

I should say, also, that we employed other field workers through the years, some of whom were Paul and Thelma Whalen, Loretta Folger, Marjorie Lammers, and Claudena Eller. This was a good program but not financially feasible for serving a large number of churches.

The Debacle of the Tabernacle

I wonder how many people still have memories of the old wood tabernacle that was the centerpiece of the International Convention held each year in Anderson, Indiana. My first memory is when I was about twelve years old. I was told the building had been erected from the left over timbers of the big World's Fair (Exposition) in St. Louis.

The buildings were for sale and some enterprising Church of God leaders had won the bid for some of the buildings. There were huge beams—many of them—and it is my understanding that some of those beams and rafters became part of the big tabernacle used primarily for the annual camp meeting. I recall that scriptures had been painted on many of the beams.

T. Franklin Miller and son, Tom; World Service Day Offering Anderson Camp Meeting

When Harold Phillips was developing skills as an amateur photographer and budding editor, he often climbed into the big rafters seeking a place for his creative camera work. Do you know Harold? I do and call him one of my dearest friends. He has suffered intense pain and heavy losses since but without apparent chafing of the shoulders and no signs of self-pity.

Harold can be a most intense person. His power to concentrate is beyond comparison. When he played handball at the local YMCA, he played to win and usually did! Handball became a passion, eventually replaced by a fascination with a camera. He became an expert. He then got interested in "ham" radio transmission, mastered the necessary skills, and participated in a worldwide network. So with everything he tried. He is an enthusiastic Rotarian, a worldwide Christian, and a dear friend.

Another word about Harold's intense concentration. He spent a weekend with us when I was pastor in Malden, Massachusetts. He took photos of our new home and of Tommy. He ate Howard Johnson's fried clams, talked, laughed, and preached. What a delightful experience. The following week I was in Anderson and at the Gospel Trumpet Company. I saw Harold coming down the hall, hands full of photos and galley proofs. I tried to stop and greet him. He simply nodded barely and walked on. That was Harold—total concentration.

Now—more about the tabernacle. The Gospel Trumpet Company owned and operated the campground. I was recording secretary of the World Service Committee and a member of the advisory committee for Gospel Trumpet Company (now Warner Press). The tabernacle had a wide almost flat roof. One night we had a heavy storm of wet snow. It accumulated on the tabernacle roof, which collapsed from the weight of the snow, leaving not much else but the four walls and the hard wooden seats. How could we even exist without the usual June campmeeting? How could we have a meeting of that size with no tabernacle or auditorium?

The snowstorm started all sorts of wheels turning. There were emergency meetings of committees and boards, including emergency meetings of the General Assembly. Many emergency decisions had to be made. There were sharply different opinions on what to do now. Robert Reardon held to one point of view. Steele Smith to another. Dr. Reardon got Judge Harold Achor, an Indiana Supreme Court judge, on the job and Steele Smith and Clarence Hatch got their advisors and lawyers.

William Eddy, pastor in Ohio, had a building contractor in his church who said he could put up a building to seat a few thousand people for only $100,000. Many of us scoffed. The power struggle was intense. Proposals and counter proposals were being bandied about. Historians have recorded the actions so I'll simply give some observations. The General Assembly eventually authorized the planning and construction of a new auditorium to seat at least 7500 people. Johnson and Ritchhart, an Anderson firm of Church of God members, were engaged as architects. The proposed auditorium was different from anything else; it would be a concrete dome raised by hydraulic jacks. The historians have that story. We have spent a fortune on that auditorium, repairing breaks, fixing acoustics, adjusting to condensation. What has not happened? It is functioning today, but at what cost? Was it necessary? Who knows?

Construction of the new building proceeded that summer. It attracted the attention of many builders and architects. Hundreds of truckloads of sand were hauled to the new site and dumped until there was what looked like a small mountain of sand. That became the form for the roof of the new building. The reinforcing rods were put in place and the entire "mountain" of sand was covered with fresh concrete. Steel posts had been put in place all around the perimeter, all fitted with hydraulic jacks. When the roof was poured and in readiness, the hydraulic lift system was put into operation. There was a large crowd of spectators. We were told this sort of construction had never been done before. The night before was chilly and the oil in the lines for the hydraulic lift was sluggish and slow to respond. After a couple of frustrating hours the sun had warmed the oil so it functioned properly. Slowly the huge concrete dome was lifted from the sand.

Later all the imported sand had to be hauled back across town and weeks of completing both exterior and interior of the dome were needed to complete the job.

When all of this was ready, a concrete floor had to be installed, the lights and sound devices put in place, and seats brought in and bolted to the floor. This was really a massive task, but finally completed.

Smile A While

I was the preacher at an Anderson College baccalaureate service in the old Park Place Church of God. This was in the original building designed according to what often was called the Akron style of architecture: square sanctuary, choir, and pulpit in one corner, and balconies on three sides. For this service, Pastor Oldham, college officials, the choir were all seated behind me, graduating seniors, faculty, and staff were on the main floor in front of me, other students, family members, and guests were in the balconies. My sermon was intended to develop the theme, "What we are to be, we are now becoming." In those days downtown Anderson had several bars and night clubs. In my sermon I said that during the previous night some fellow got drunk in one of these establishments and was arrested and put in jail. I meant to say, "Today that man is in his jail cell, holding his head in a painful hangover." What I said was, "This morning that man is sitting in his sale jell." I doubt if any of the graduating seniors or faculty members were even listening to me, and they missed my blunder. Pastor Oldham, others on the platform, and most of the people in the balconies all burst out laughing. I laughed heartily. Doctor Oldham stepped over, put his arm around my shoulder, laughed, and said, "Go ahead, Brother Miller, we all know where the drunken man was." Laughter, robust or mild, often eases the tensions, so we relax and move on with our journey.

Spiritual Disciplines and the Journey

There is another aspect of the Journey that should be mentioned, although it is very personal. I refer to the day by day observance of spiritual disciplines.

The Bible is of primary significance. I am a preacher, so I read the Bible from the perspective of a preacher, always alert to scripture that would be helpful for expository preaching and texts for sermonic treatment. I doubt that many preachers ignore this discipline.

There is another approach of scripture reading and that is to read the Bible in a devotional mood. For many years Gertie and I have deliberately set out to read the Bible through in this fashion. We keep several versions at the breakfast table and often read a passage from more than one version. Sometimes I keep a Bible commentary handy to help get a better understanding of the Scripture. We usually read from the Revised Standard Version, and often we would use a yellow highlighter pen to underline favorite passages. When we were not engaged in reading the Bible through, we would read favorite passages from the Psalms or some of the letters of Paul. We have often turned to a passage we had underlined and talked about the particular time and circumstance when that scripture had helped us in a special way. We still do that. Often we have used the scripture that was the basis for a sermon by our pastor.

We have enriched this experience further by singing from the hymnal words that helped to reinforce the Scripture we read. Sometimes the song or chorus comes first then we read the appropriate scripture. A few times we added further enrichment by playing a recording. Seasonal music is especially helpful. We have often tied our devotional reading to a text from which I am going to preach or it could be after I have preached on a text.

Both of us are helped by the use of devotional thoughts taken from current magazine readings or from books by favorite authors. Sometimes we read from an anthology of inspirational and devotional writings. Both Gertie and I are members of small prayer groups that often add new enrichment or dimension to our own prayer and study. We feel so at home in this part of our journey, it can be so meaningful and helpful.

I have frequently referred to the effective use of personal islands of peace and inspiration. I once used this metaphor as a means of personal spiritual renewal and a writer who was present in the group I was leading pursued it further. He wrote personal letters to two hundred world and national leaders and after explaining the idea of islands of peace and renewal of perspective and inspiration, he asked for comments on what they did for such renewal. He received replies from about one hundred and seventy-five persons. All of them affirmed that, of course, they had used islands of peace and renewal and went on to describe their "islands." These were all persons of national or international repute and influence—political leaders, professional persons, business leaders. For many of us, like these leaders, islands of peace and renewal are the part of the journey that is most necessary for creative and effective living in situation of tension, problems, calling for courage and boldness often in adversity and pain.

For almost a lifetime I have combined gardening with cultivating a devotional life. I have found in much of my gardening a time and place for creative meditation. In this sense the journey really is my home. Here is an illustration from a recent experience.

Gertie and I had used Psalm 18, devotionally; it describes God's loving care for us by many metaphors: "With God's help I can scale a wall." "He pulled me out of the miry clay." "He set my feet on a solid rock." "He broadened the path before me so my ankles do not turn." Those and similar thoughts are in my mind as on a typical day I get a shovel, rake, hoe, pruning cutters, and so forth. Today I will work on the roses and the message of Psalm 18 is vivid in my mind. I meditate on it while I am busy with pruning shears and I visualize a mountain path, meadow, and rocky. I smooth a spot near one of my favorite rose bushes as I put both feet flat on the ground and balance carefully. I recall that not long ago I had lost my balance in a similar situation and almost sprained my ankle. Quite consciously I test the safety of the place where I stand and thank the Lord for solid footing. I remember the passages in Psalm 18 when I almost fell into the rose bush and how the thorns tore at my legs. I consciously give thanks for God's protection that saved me from the rose thorns.

The weather is conducive to further reflection and I meditate several times in the same spot where I almost lost my balance and almost fell into the bushes of roses and thorns. I have developed several possibly good sermons in this spot where I almost fell into thorns. I am humbled and meditate more on God's loving protection.

Smile A While

Many congregations of the Church of God, perhaps most of them, observe the washing of feet as a religious act of worship. In one church, a member lived too far away to attend regularly, and he missed many of the church events that he really wanted to attend. Once he did arrange to be present when foot washing was being practiced. In a later service when others were sharing their testimonies, he arose and said, "My brothers and sisters, I thank you and I thank the Lord that I finally got my feet washed." Who wouldn't see some humor in that?

Some Travel Memories

Travel is a necessary part of the life of any church agency executive. It became a large part of my life. I traveled an average of 100,000 miles a year. There were rewards to travel, and there were problems. Since I had to travel every year, Gertie and I tried to make the best of our situation. When I could drive and take our family with me we often went together. The disadvantage was that we had losses by not being home for special programs and special events with Tom and Sue and friends at church and school. One advantage was that we would be together as a family. We visited many places not possible otherwise and at little cost to us.

Family included trips were usually on weekends, school vacations, and during summer months. This was an integral part of the "journey." I will record here a few of my memories with Sue, Tom, and Gertie. There is no attempt at correct time sequence. On all our trips we had lots of fun, we hope we did good to someone, and we came closer as a family.

On some of the longer trips when we stayed in a motel, we often bought fruit and dry cereal, milk, and rolls. We had a small cooler in the car to keep fruit and milk, plastic dishes, and spoons. We ate breakfast in the motel and washed "dishes" there.

As I recall it, one trip always brings feelings of guilt. We were going to the Minnesota Youth Camp where I had program responsibilities, and also to a long weekend with Pastor and Board Member Russell Shield. Sue and Tom each packed a suitcase. Sue very dutifully packed her clothing, locked her case, and left it on her bed. I did not see it and later felt horribly guilty. (Please forgive me, Sue.) Before we got to our destination, we discovered my error. We called my mother, who was living with us, and asked her to have Sue's suitcase mailed to us by American Express. Meanwhile, we stopped and bought Sue some clothes.

At the youth camp there was a slide into the pool and all swimmers used it. I was so proud of Tom and Sue for being good swimmers and so ashamed that I couldn't. For a few days after the camp we stayed at a motel on a lake. We caught many perch but all were diseased so we did not keep them. On that trip we walked across the Mississippi on a footbridge at the river's source. Later that year we drove across the same river on the long bridge at Memphis, Tennessee, and later a longer bridge near New Orleans. We learned something of geography on every trip.

Once we all went to New Orleans, where I had responsibility for the "Institute" for black pastors. Almost every day we drove to a lake to see the swans. On the way home, just outside Birmingham, Alabama, we stopped at a roadside "show" for each child to take a pony ride and all to get ice cream cones.

Clara Smith's father, John Lorton, a successful Florida pastor, made possible two or three trips to Florida. On one trip we picked oranges and grapefruit to bring home, and the morning we left, discovered Sue had chicken pox. With permission of the owner we spent one night at a motel coming home and stopped for "carry out meals" to eat in the car. She had no long-term ill effects.

One Mother's Day weekend we left for Springfield, Illinois, where I was to speak the next day. We explored a lot of Lincoln lore. We got corsages for each of us for the next day but no one else in the church had any.

On a Florida trip we went on the sponge boats and watched divers gather sponges. Both children spent several days playing in sand on the beach. On that same trip to Florida, before we got to our destination, we ran into severe hail. I could see the road only with difficulty, afraid to stop and afraid to continue. Gertie was in the front seat with me, praying, and Tom and Sue chattering, almost shouting, in the back seat. The hail hit the car with force and made a horrible noise and expensive dents. Gertie turned to Sue and Tom and asked them to be quiet. Sue asked, "Why?" Since the hail made so much noise we could hardly hear each other shout.

On a long trip to the Northwest we had not made motel reservations and before dark we learned our mistake. There were many motels, but all were full. Finally we joined thirty-five or more other cars of tourists and spent the night sleeping(?) in a large gas station; it opened at 6:00 A.M. for late comers like us to use toilets and car service. What a long day for the driver. We stopped at a quiet motel and found a small stream in back. I got some string and made fish hooks out of safety pins and Tom and Sue each caught some small fish that were too small to keep but good for catching.

On this trip we explored the Badlands of South Dakota, saw the presidents of Mount Rushmore, ate a delicious lunch there, stopped at other mountain resorts, and went to Yellowstone National Park. Tom and I fished for trout at famed fishing bridge in the lake (no trout). Later we learned how to catch them and drove on through the colorful west: In western Washington, at the church campgrounds; Oregon campmeeting, on south to Santa Rosa (home of Charles Shultz) leader's camp with Tom and Clara Smith, then south through Bakersfield and the desert (slept at midnight for two hours on the ground of the courthouse lawn) to the Grand Canyon for breakfast. We were too sleepy to be aware and finally found a motel with a swimming pool. Tom and Sue and the Smiths enjoyed the pool, but Gertie and I slept!

When Tom was still in elementary school, he flew with me to Boston for a few days of meeting with Albert Donaldson, then pastor at the Everett Church. He always had a dog, sometimes more than one. Al had convinced me that Tom should have a dog, and he had a couple to sell. We bought a cocker spaniel and rode home in a car with Steele Smith. He fumed all the way because we did not know how to care for the dog. The dog was a beautiful creature. We learned he had an ear infection. One day he disappeared. We think someone stole him. Much later Tom and I learned how to care for a dog and got "Nappy" (for Napoleon), a white loving and loved dog. Pages could be written about Nappy. He was loved by all neighbor children. He was later loved by the Anderson University students whom he helped cheer at football games. "Get that white dog off the field and keep him off!" the referee would say. "Tom, get Nappy!" said 500 students.

One summer we rented a cabin across a lake from a summer music camp in Michigan. My mother was with us. In the evening we left Nappy on a screened in back porch while we drove around the lake to enjoy a free concert. Wonderful. We got back to find what sport Nappy had by tearing up Tom's sleeping bag (into 1,000 pieces). We got new gear and watched Nappy closely after that. I took my mother in a boat on the lake and she fished and got many blue gills. She was elated—but I had to clean them.

On one western trip we had written confirmed reservations at a beach house in Carpenteria, California, but the host had no record of it. We finally got a place to stay and had a delightful three or four days on the beach. On that trip we stopped in the afternoon for ice cream. The waitress did not bring Gertie hers. Gertie said, "It's okay, don't worry about me!" That expression has endured in our family. Like many people, we have a lot of favorite expressions, each one recalling some unusual experience.

The summer of Sue's sixteenth birthday was quite a summer for us. The International Youth Convention of the Church of God was to be in Edmonton, Alberta, Canada, and I carried administrative responsibilities for it. Esther Bauer was our national children's director, and Edith Lindenman was office manager as well as my special administrative assistant. Tom was in college and he and three others went on a quartet tour (promotion for Anderson College) to the southwest, up the west coast, to Canada, and the convention. Gertie and I put it all together. We arranged for Esther to drive and take Edith with her, visit the northwest and Canada churches, promote children's and Christian education work, and Edith would be at the youth convention for administrative leadership.

Sue's best friends, Connie Reardon, Barbara Falls, and Barbara Long, were all gone for the summer. Alan Egly, youth director, planned a special tour by train from Chicago to Edmonton, exclusively for convention youth. We paid some in advance, and I carried with me a cashier's check for the balance of several thousands in American dollars.

Gertie, Sue, and I would fly to Seattle, Washington, spend a couple of days at the World's Fair, and vacation a few days in Western Canada. From Seattle we flew to Vancouver, British Columbia, Canada, and then two nights on the Victoria Island, British Columbia. Victoria is more British than London. We had a wonderful visit. Then we flew back to Calgary, rented a red Chevrolet convertible, and spent two nights at the Chateau on Lake Louise. This was all sheer luxury and we could not afford it. Could I ever make it up to Tom and be fair? Sue's birthday dinner at "The Chateau" was extra special. (I hope she still remembers it!) I let her drive the convertible (top down and Gertie in the back seat) wind blowing cold. I knew Esther and Edith were traveling near by and surely enough we found them. We followed a mile or so, then with Sue driving (horn blasting) she passed them. What sheer adolescent thrills for all of us.

We got back to Calgary and on to Edmonton. Alan had all things in order (as always) and we were set for a rewarding experience. I walked across the street to the big bank, ready to pay for a return train to Chicago for our 200 or 300 young people. I got to the bank president and he refused to take my cashier's cheek. What dismay and panic. In a strange country—being refused like a common thief. I had documentation to show I was a director of Anderson Banking Company and former president of Chamber of Commerce in Anderson, Indiana. No use! Impasse! Finally the banker asked if I would pay for a personal phone call to Mr. Wilbur Roby, President of Anderson Banking Company. I agreed quickly. He placed the call and in a few minutes all was cleared and my money was good. Then he showed me my picture in his top-drawer file—a bank robber and swindler, who had robbed many Canadean banks of cashier's checks, forged signatures, and more. I was the thief, still loose but wanted by Canada's Royal Mounted Police. The photo was like my twin. What relief—finally! We settled all financial affairs and I had clearance to leave. We had a marvelous convention. I was free. At the close of the convention we drove home with Esther and Edith, not the world's happiest people, but alive and free. Tom had car trouble but a fine trip.

One summer Tom, Sandy, and Scott had reservations for a week at the famous Hilton Head resort in South Carolina and arranged for us to join them. Tom had tee times reserved for great golf. The day before we left home I accidentally swung my hand into the stair railing at home and broke my finger. So much for my golf. I felt we would only be extra baggage for Tom and Sandy, but we went ahead with our plans.

At the resort I saw many boys and girls fishing in shallow water while adults golfed. So Scott and I went to a store and got some fishing tackle and he and I fished from a bank near our cottage. To our surprise he got a good strike and carefully pulled in a twenty-two inch spotted bass! We were elated, but a crocodile had also seen the fish and followed it in. I was scared. Scott and I both ran into the house. We got a good photo of the fish but none of the crocodile. Since then Scott and I have caught a lot of other fish, but none that almost cost an arm and a leg, or our lives!

The rest of the trip home was a nightmare. I had car trouble. Tom, Sandy, and our grandson, Scott, were getting ready to move to Kansas City and I stubbornly insisted on getting our car fixed so I could help them pack books. I apologize, Tom and Sandy, please forgive. I now know I ruined for Tom and Sandy what could have been a delightful memory. I know it mattered to Scott. I wish I could forget my stubborn refusal to let Tom and Sandy fly home, get their packing done, and Gertie and I could have had a safe trip instead of the necessary speeding and dangerous driving. I hope to forget that part of life's journey.

One time our granddaughter Gwen reminded me I had taken Scott fishing but had not taken her. I was glad for her honesty but regretted my oversight. Sue and Spencer were living in Michigan, courtesy of a preacher who became and remains a dear friend, now retired in Port Huron, Michigan. I did some checking and found a stocked lake nearby. So Gwen and I packed some fruit and sandwiches and went fishing! We enjoyed our roadside lunch and then found our lake. It was great fishing! Gwen caught several trout. We paid for them, had them cleaned, and ate them for supper.

Fishing with our granddaughter Christy was different. We found a farm in northern Indiana—a real working dairy farm—that also took in guests. Christy and Gwen were given a large ground floor bedroom and Gertie and I were in a large upstairs room in another part of the house. It was not long until the girls came into our room, somewhat frightened! We understood. The three women climbed into one bed and I made a bed on the floor. We all slept soundly.

The next morning we had a real "country" farm breakfast and explored the dairy barn and farm. Gwen won the love of the farmer. He let her ride a horse. It was thrilling for her.

Christy and I found a fishing rod and line in the barn and a safe spot on the bank of the farmer's pond. We dug here and there and found a couple of worms (one was enough.) I cast the line out with a bobber on and gave it to Christy. She could hardly hold the pole but held on and as we looked we saw her bobber go under. She wound the reel, held on, kept reeling, and pulled in a big twenty-inch bass. The farmer cleaned it and we had a fish dinner for supper. What fun I have had just trying to make a meaningful memory for a grandchild. The journey is not only our home. Parts of it are delicious, fun, delightful, joyous, and remarkable. I hope the grandchildren really enjoy some of these memories.

One year Gertie and I had the idea of asking her sister, Lettie, who lived in Maryland, to spend a few days with us on a trip where our son Tom lived. She agreed. She flew with us to Portland, Oregon, we got our grandson, and the four of us drove to the Pacific Coast and then south on Route 1 along the Pacific Coast. Neither Scott nor Lettie had ever seen a redwood tree. We spent hours in the Santa Rosa, California grove, taking pictures, just trying to absorb the wonder and beauty of the trees. We drove further the next day or so, but finally had to go back to Portland. We had a delightful and thrilling few days together. We were always glad we had a chance to provide this for Lettie. How wonderful if we could have given a trip like this to our parents! We thanked God for the present joy of creating some lifetime memories for us and our family.

IX

Smile A While

A long time ago an untrained song leader was leading the singing in a large summer tabernacle with a metal roof. Outside it was raining. The song he chose was "Reigning in this life," a song we sang with enthusiasm in those days. He heard rain drops hitting the metal roof and did not understand the difference between reigning and raining. We young people thought it was funny but did not dare laugh in church!

Music on the Journey

Music is central to our family life. It could also be said that music is an integral part of the journey. In my own family we had a piano; my sister, Icy, played it. My sister, Ocy, and I each played a saxophone. I played a guitar. Howard played a slide trombone and sang in a high school quartet and the chorale. We had a family quartet: Icy—soprano; Ocy—alto; I—tenor; my father—bass. We sang hymns and "special songs" in church.

Gertie has a beautiful high soprano voice. In Baltimore she studied voice at the Peabody Conservatory. After we were married she continued private voice lessons in Boston and later in Indianapolis. I always felt guilty that she could not continue those lessons.

Early in life we found that Tom had perfect pitch in music. He started taking piano lessons from Charlotte Brooks before he was five years old. Piano music seemed to come naturally to Sue. It was amazing what she could play by ear. Tom needed the music on paper, and she didn't. Sue would be playing and Tom would call out from another part of the house, "Sue, that is a B flat!" Tom majored in music in college and traveled with a male quartet.

Sue had many invitations to provide background piano music for luncheons and dinners. It seemed she could play for a couple of hours and not repeat. Before she got to college she was also learning to play the organ.

The first record player we had came with only classical recordings and we played and played "Dance of the Flowers." How then did Tom become so enamored of and proficient in jazz? Dr. Paul Brietweiser was Tom's mentor and idol. Dr. Brietweiser did not seem to be bothered. He said Tom would outgrow it. I don't think he has, but he has appreciation for many kinds of music and we learned to appreciate real jazz.

Once in later years, Tom was going to be visiting for a few days in Anderson with us. Gertie asked if there was someone Tom would like to invite to dinner. Tom, without hesitation, asked for Dr. Paul, who had given his life to teaching children and young people elementary music. What a high calling Paul made of that. So have Sue and Tom and Sandy—all of them in their performance of music—church, vocal solo and duet, pipe organ, and piano, choir directing, composing, and arranging. To a large degree our three grandchildren share these same interests and some aptitude in music.

Tom has moved on to be immediate Past President of the Northwest Chapter of American Choral Director's Association. His Warner Pacific Choir has become well known for their excellence in music. Tom also leads a chamber choir named "Novum Cantorum" that gives several concerts a year to standing-room-only audiences. They are semi-pro musicians. Sue could be the full time organist at any one of Anderson's top ten churches if she wanted to. Sandy's youth ensemble and children's choir have sung, by invitation, at England's Canterbury Festival and Carnegie Hall in New York City. Music is a part of us—and of the journey.

Smile A While

A dear friend and trusted colleague of mine was Miss Lottie Franklin; the "Franklin" in both of our names is sometimes confusing. Lottie and I were sharing leadership at a church conference. I had to leave before the meeting closed, but as I was getting my hat and coat I heard a woman in the audience say, "Miss Franklin, I would like further comments on the statement your husband made just before he left a few minutes ago." Lottie smiled and said she never had a husband.

Park Place Church of God

In the mid 1940s Dr. E. A. Reardon was pastor of the Park Place Church of God in Anderson, Indiana. Gertrude Little was director of Christian education. There was also a stenographer who served as a personal secretary to the pastor.

I was a high school teacher in our church Sunday school with Mrs. Ida Byrd Rowe and William Bowser, Sr. I was named a member of the Park Place Church of God Board of Christian Education and then chairman of that Board. **Bessie Byrum** had served as Sunday school superintendent and was still a powerful force in that part of church life.

Gertrude Little, our church director of Christian education, had few living relatives. She earned a doctor's degree in Christian education; she stood almost alone as a leader in this part of the church life. She suffered from not having a clear written position description giving the parameters of her position in the Park Place Church. How often she called me to clarify some aspect of her work and usually worked in the phrase, "I never know what my responsibilities are and don't know the limits of my authority." She lived out in front. She was not afraid to tackle a new job, yet she usually seemed to have second thoughts about her decisions. She was well read in all the latest books and theories in the field.

Once she got enamored of giving every teacher a year's leave of absence, and asked me as chairman, to notify teachers of their upcoming leave. I did not find one teacher who was happy with this "enforced" sabbatical; they all resented it. Tressie McCreary was one such person. When I tried to explain the plan to her she could not understand it. She taught juniors and I thought did very well. She was offended at the thought of a year's sabbatical. She was a sister to Bessie Byrum. We had things all set for a first class church fight. I finally won by getting the board to rescind its action and forget the whole business. Either way, my popularity was not increased!

Gertrude introduced the "worship folder" for Sunday morning, against much protest. It lived anyway. She introduced the annual teacher evaluation scale and the public dedication of teachers. She also started the annual all-day retreat for Christian education workers featuring a guest speaker. She also taught at Anderson University.

When Dale Oldham was pastor, he brought in Carl Swart as Christian education leader. Carl was not academically qualified for the position, and there were frequent conflicts over his leadership.

Arlene Hall was an able administrator in this field. The national Board of Christian Education had employed her. When I was executive secretary, she applied for and was accepted for graduate studies at Scarrett College in Nashville, Tennessee. In our office we were so glad for her. She asked if she would have a job when she finished and I told her no. Instead, she worked at Warner Press, and then came to Park Place Church as director of Christian education.

Arlene led the way to establishing a nursery school at Park Place. It was fully accredited by the State of Indiana from the first. Velma Smith (Mrs. J. Edgar Smith), Ethel Phillips, and Dorothy Nicholson were the other moving spirits that pioneered in this venture. It has been first class from the very first day and a model for many similar ventures. Arlene became well known, also, for her written prayers given Sunday morning worship.

As chair of the Board of Christian Education, I usually learned in advance the names of persons being considered as teachers or other leadership positions. I always gave these names in advance to the pastor and got his approval before they came to the board.

Dorothy Nicholson served so well in this whole area of Christian education. She took ministry to children another step forward in establishing After School Fun and the Children's Center. How blessed we are at Park Place to have so many eminently qualified persons to serve in so many places.

Anita Womack stepped in to serve as an associate pastor for Christian education. She also enriched our lives as she led in prayer in many Sunday morning services, and then gave printed copies to all in the congregation. Her untimely death cut short a courageous and fruitful pastoral ministry with emphasis on children's work.

For many years Lottie Franklin very effectively filled the role of leader of adult Christian education in our church. She, like the others, was constantly searching for more volunteer leaders and teachers.

In these years Robert Nicholson and I teamed as teachers of a college age Sunday school class. We met in the most unlikely room for a class—the Boy Scout room. It had poor ventilation and poorer acoustics, but Nick and I capitalized on all the deficiencies and built an average attendance of near ninety every Sunday, using true team teaching. We planned our lessons in units, usually four to six, and one of us had primary responsibility for the unit. Both of us enjoyed using a wide variety of teaching methods. We used them all—lecture, role-play, interaction, special reports, debates, visiting leaders, audio visuals, and so forth. Never a dull moment!

Dorothy Nicholson and Gertie often helped in our teaching, and several times every year planned a huge supper party held in our home or the Nicholson's that was always a great success. I enjoyed this period of the journey. It was stimulating and rewarding to work with Nick and Dorothy. What fun! Before the new church building was erected we met in a variety of places—old Park Place School, private homes, the huge basement of Bill Bowser's house, for example.

Planning for classrooms was a huge part of the work for the new building we eventually constructed. In addition to my work as Christian education chairman, I was secretary of the building committee for a long time.

This meant studying space requirements for all classes, projecting plans for the future, and studying state and national space and facility requirements. The result was a building made to last, adaptable, useable, flexible. It is excellent.

Serving as secretary of the building committee meant not only my keeping accurate records of all proceedings, but an examination of all plans and proposals so they fit our needs. Sometimes this called for very detailed examinations.

Dedication of Land, Park Place Church of God
Ray Tuttle, Milton Buettner, Dale Oldham, T. Franklin Miller

When Dr. Oldham was pastor, people began calling for a Pastor's Advisory Committee; eventually a church council was formed, and I was named chairman. We met monthly and most often in a private home. Frequently we met at the home of Everett and Ersel Hartung, who were always gracious hosts. We received requests from the pastor for clarification of items in his work and suggestions for church improvement.

The monthly *Christian Century* published a service called "Great Churches of America." We were given the assignment to examine them and bring at least one good idea from each church that would make Park Place a better church. It was a very productive discipline and went over several months.

We also gave guidance in selecting members of the pastoral staff and prepared recommendations for salary administration. In this I served every year. We had council members who were also Anderson University faculty or staff, and they seemed always to compare proposals with their own assignments and salary. It was always a problem, and I felt for years that the college people were unfairly comparing incomes and workloads. Much of our energy was focused on getting adequate staff.

When Dr. Oldham began giving so much energy to the Christian Brotherhood Hour, we had more problems with people who felt he was neglecting parts of his role as pastor. This was never really resolved to satisfaction.

When Keith Huttenlocker was pastor, there was a call for a careful study of the church organization. Some professional help was used, sometimes to my irritation. Finally we agreed on some principles and after much re-working (and a lot of money) developed a design for ministry which served fairly well for a while, until people began using it as a legal document rather than a set of guidelines for our work. It has been redone.

In the design we called for a Staff Parish Relations Committee. I have served my share of time in this role, as have several others.

We developed some guidelines for performance evaluation and in proposing salary and benefits. This committee was also supposed to hear any complaints related to staff persons. It was never easy. It is difficult to be objective in these matters.

I owe so much to the Park Place Church of God. I held revival meetings here under the pastoral leadership of Dr. Reardon and Dr. Oldham. I have been given many opportunities to serve: I have taught Sunday school classes from juniors through adults, and chaired the board of Christian education for many years. I was the first official chair of the church council, secretary of the building committee, and often a fund-raiser. I have served a full term as chair of the staff-parish relations committee. In each position, I have gained much more than I have given, and each one for me was an experience of learning and growth. I am humbled and profoundly grateful for the earnest prayers from this congregation, spoken for me during times of illness, distress, and crucial decisions. I have loved and supported all our pastors from Dr. Gray to Dr. Markle. Gertie and I have deep affection for this congregation; it is unique and it is home to us. Now and then we hear some criticism, but it comes from those who will grow and learn. I have visited congregations all over this country, have preached in more than thirteen hundred of them, and would not trade the loving fellowship of this redeemed and redeeming community for any dozen or more of the others that I have visited.

Smile A While

Doctor Estel Perry, when he was a pastor and chairperson of the national Board of Christian Education, handsome with his wavy black hair and dearly loved by all who knew him, was asked to give the prayer at a large area meeting in Detroit, Michigan. The person in charge had suggested that Dr. Perry close by calling for unison repeating of the Lord's Prayer. His tongue also got twisted and he started what should have been a unison prayer with, "The Lord is my shepherd...." The audience was silent, so he said it again, "Let us pray the prayer our Lord taught us, 'The Lord is my shepherd, I shall not....'" He realized something was wrong, so he tried it the third time and made the same mistake again. He shook his head in distress and sat down. We know how he felt, don't we? Can we laugh at ourselves as he did when he told the story on himself?

Christian Brotherhood Hour (Church of God)

Dr. Dale Oldham will always be known not only as the pastor of the Park Place Church of God, Anderson Indiana, but also as the founder of the Christian Brotherhood Hour (CBH). It was first a dream, then a reality. Dr. Oldham had developed a radio broadcasting style from his years of reporting the evening news while he was also pastor in Dayton, Ohio. He had a rich baritone voice and knew how to use it. He also developed unusual skill in preparing and reading from a manuscript. He learned how to fit a broadcast into a specific time frame. His skill enabled him to read the manuscript without appearing to read it. He could speak spontaneously but through the discipline of writing a manuscript, he carefully chose his words so the message was relevant and to the point.

In Anderson he became closely associated with Richard Meiskhe, an Anderson College graduate who had honed his skills in fine radio broadcasting.

All of this was priceless in fulfilling a dream of a religious radio program prepared in advance and taped for simultaneous broadcast on several radio stations. Robert Nicholson of Anderson College formed a chorale of mostly Anderson College students for music in the program. They became the Christian Brotherhood Hour Choralaires. It was not long until a CBH male quartet became a regular feature. This was at first composed of Doug Oldham, Ronald Patty, Paul Clausen (until his illness made a change necessary), and Ernest Gross. Dick Miesche changed his name to Richard Lee and continued in radio (and later) television production.

Dr. Oldham became acquainted with Jack O'Dell who had experienced a remarkable conversion from alcoholism. Jack had almost lost his career in radio production and had a moving testimony to the redeeming love of God. He and Dale became close friends and colleagues.

I have vivid memories of the first CBH broadcast. It was taped and scheduled for airing on a Sunday afternoon over a local Anderson station. I was chairman of the Park Place Church Council; we called a congregational meeting for the Sunday afternoon premier performance. We set up a radio in our sanctuary and gathered for sharing this historic occasion. It was moving and wonderful.

From the first day, Dr. Harold Phillips, editor of *Vital Christianity*, carried Dr. Oldham's weekly sermon in the magazine. Listeners were told how to get a free copy of the week's sermon. This boosted circulation for *Vital Christianity* and increased support for the broadcast.

Dr. Oldham encouraged listeners to write to him about the message, for prayer requests, or reaction to the program. That called for a mailing address and the Board of Church Extension and Home Missions became the official sponsor of CBH, which also meant that donation checks were made payable to and sent to the Board of Church Extension. At first all parties were happy with this arrangement. Dr. Oldham answered all the correspondence, at first using the secretarial service of the Park Place Church of God; then it was moved to the office of the Board of Church Extension. Dr. Oldham naturally felt he had a vested interest in the correspondence, and it was not long until this growing list of CBH listeners received a promotional fund raising letter from Dr. Oldham.

The next step was to be expected. Dr. Oldham and Dick Lee wanted an accounting of income and expenses and some financial control over the operation. The Board of Church Extension was reluctant to grant this. Conversations and negotiations continued but were unsuccessful.

Many persons were involved in this controversy. Dr. E. F. Adcock was the chief executive officer of the Board of Church Extension. Dr. W. H. Hunt was chair of the board. Some other board members were Earl Martin, Oscar Flynt, and Steele Smith. All of these were also members of the Park Place Church of God and, therefore, Dr. Oldham's parishioners. In those days the general agencies of the church had a lot of overlapping of board membership which resulted in a network of interlocking persons and programs.

Dr. Oldham and Dick Meiskhe both felt an urgent need to send out some promotional fund raising literature and decided they would not ever get the mailing list just for the asking. One dark night they went into the Church Extension office and removed all the files and data related to the CBH broadcast.

The next day—and for many days after—this was the only topic of discussion in Church of God circles. Dr. Adcock and Dr. Hunt called it an evil and uncalled for act of thievery. The CBH people said they took only what was rightfully theirs. The tension and ill will cannot be described. On Sunday Pastor Dale rose to preach; sitting in front of him were people who had lost confidence in his integrity. The rift widened. People took sides—for or against their own pastor. Both sides held strongly that they were in the right. In those hours, Park Place Church came as close as it ever would to a major split. Many people were trying to mediate and bring peace and understanding.

Dr. Earl Martin, a highly respected Anderson College professor and former president of the Board of Church Extension, came to me with a suggestion. He recalled that in National Leaders' Camps we had times of renewal through prayer and confession. He suggested we invite to our house many of the persons involved in this strange situation that had now paralyzed our work so that the issues could be resolved in prayer and humility. I agreed to send out the invitations to a dozen or so. All came. Dale was late and, when he came, Polly, his wife, was with him. That was delicate. I explained that these were all men, so Dale walked Polly home (up the street just a block or so). When he returned Dr. Martin read passages from the New Testament, and we sang "Let Me See Jesus Only" and "Just a Closer Walk with

Thee." Then we knelt in prayer. Several prayed, but not Pastor Dale. When we rose he expressed his own disappointment that we did not trust him and insisted he was in the right in his action as leader of CBH. The issue was never fully resolved but no changes were made at that time.

Much later CBH came under the umbrella of the Radio and Television Commission and the program has now grown to a place of worldwide leadership, powerful influence, and trusted support.

I recall when Pastor Dale sought my counsel about his work and CBH. It was consuming vast time and energies. Almost every week he traveled somewhere for a CBH Rally. Either Marvin Hartman or I stood ready to fill his pulpit on Sunday morning if he was delayed. Several times I stood just off the platform, Bible and sermon in one hand, the other hand on the door, when pastor arrived at the last second. That was not fun.

Anyway, I told Dale he was at a crossroads and had to decide whether to give up CBH to pastor the church or resign and go full time in radio work. He chose to leave. He left with our love and loyalty as many of us tried to blank out the memory of the big rift in relationships. He was a great man, a powerful preacher, and one I loved.

Two Dear Women and a Man

My mother and Mrs. E. A. Reardon were about the same size and both held firmly to religious convictions. Mrs. Reardon's eyes were dark brown, my mother's blue. Both believed in divine healing—only Mrs. Reardon would be less hesitant to call a doctor in time of need. Both had two sons; my mother also had two daughters. Dr. E. A. Reardon was pastor of Park Place Church of God; my father operated a metal lathe in the Rock Island Railroad shops. Both women had love and compassion and eagerly used their skills in church work.

Everett Hartung was a leading lay person at the Park Place Church of God. Rumor was that Everett had taken bankruptcy. I know a few people helped spread that and other rumors but that did not deter his enthusiasm for Park Place Church of God nor his generosity. He became a dear friend. His white hair was beautiful, his blue eyes warm and kind, his handshake firm, and his generosity boundless.

During two particularly difficult times, Mrs. Reardon was compassionately helpful. After Sue was born, Gertie had a mild clinical depression. Two Park Place women came to pray for her—"to cast out the devils"—and Mrs. Reardon put a stop to their efforts. She surrounded Gertie with love and wisdom. Bless her! Dean Olt helped us get specialized medical treatment for Gertie and she gained new self-esteem and improved health.

When my mother's cancer was growing, Dr. Charles Armington called on us. He always went upstairs to see my mother. I can hear him now begging her to let him care for the growing sore on her arm. She refused. It got worse and grew to be a large cancer. She got weaker and required constant care—which Gertie freely and graciously gave.

One day after weeks of distress, mother told me I could now take her to the hospital. She said she was ready to die. I took her. Dr. Armington and Dr. James Doenges amputated the right arm at the elbow. My mother had expected to die, but she awakened surprised that she was still alive. I had made arrangements to stay until her surgery was completed, when Mrs. Reardon entered the room. After prayer she said, "Now I am staying, so you go on about your work. Run along now!" I did. She stayed and helped over many days and nights. How could Gertie or I forget that kind of a woman?

There's more. St. John's Hospital expected all bills to be paid weekly. We had scrimped and saved enough for a down payment on my mother's surgery since she did not have medical insurance. When I went to pay, the clerk was confused. She looked at different forms. All was paid. Later I found that Everett Hartung had used his influence to get all the medical bills paid or covered. How can we forget that kind of love?

National Leaders' Camps

A phenomena of the 1940s in the Church of God were the national Leaders Camps. Irene Smith Caldwell was leading the National Board of Christian Education as its executive secretary when the first camp was held—this one at Camp Jennings, Missouri. In a few months Irene married Mark Caldwell and moved to Portland, Oregon. The work of Christian education would be continued temporarily by the leadership of R. Eugene Sterner soon to be followed by T. Franklin

Miller. A. Leland Forrest was leaving the leadership of the national youth fellowship, soon to be followed by Leslie Decker and Tom A. Smith. These persons were influenced by retreats for leaders such as The Ashrams led by Dr. E. Stanley Jones, missionary to India, the Camps Farthest Out by Dr. Glenn Clark, and similar other retreats for spiritual renewal and those questing for a more effective lifestyle in leadership.

With roots such as these, the camps soon developed their own unique style in leadership, and by group consent soon brought forth certain guidelines. In an informal camp setting some seventy-five or more persons were nominated for participation in these camps. A deliberate balance was sought in age (young, middle age, and older), men and women, known theological positions (conservative vs. liberal, autocratic vs. democratic, historic creedal statements vs. non structured free-flowing creative positions). We tried to keep attendance interracial. Cost was determined by camp rental and meals. There was a subsidy by the national board. Travel for leaders was usually absorbed by their agency budgets. Participating program persons could be given a modest honorarium.

These "rules" were agreed on: Everyone attends all sessions. A point of view may be expressed freely—with no visible "judgment." The Bible was read and studied for devotional values. A leadership team of five or six persons handled all program matters, by consensus when possible. Informal dress always; no neckties allowed. No criticism—spoken or implied.

Leaders' Camp Gathering

Each day in a "family" meeting, an hour would be given for suggestions and questions. The days would close around a campfire. One person was asked to suggest a word for the day, such as *church, Bible, fellowship, forgiveness.*

After the first night we would observe "corporate silence," whose purpose was to listen to one's inner voice and the voice of God. The silence would be broken the next morning at worship. Before breakfast, all gathered outdoors, each with Bible and paper and pen.

A prenamed leader would break the silence with a scripture. This contained a strong affirmation that would be used as we greeted each other during the day. Here are a couple of examples: Bible: "I will lift up my eyes to the hills..."; affirmation: "I will lift up everything." Bible: "I can do all things through Christ." affirmation— "Christ is my total strength." Through the day we would often repeat the affirmation.

A major presentation was given between 10:00 to 11:00 A.M. One year this was on the ministry of the Holy Spirit. The same themes were used each morning for a week with one speaker. One year Harold Phillips spoke on the life of Paul. He highlighted current problems—such as the place of women, social justice, and relations with brothers and sisters who differ, and so forth. One year I spoke on the life of Christ. At the close of the presentation one could say, "I would like to pursue further discussion of.… At 2:00 o'clock I will be at the big oak tree, (or wherever) and will gladly have dialogue with anyone who wants it."

The afternoon was free—hike, sleep, Bible study, conversations, and so forth. Mealtimes—lots of fun, light humor, light folk singing, led by the chosen leaders. This was followed with a Family Meeting. A "Papa and Mama" were named to lead. This was an open meeting for any suggestion, or constructive criticism.

After supper, camp fire and fellowship took place, followed by bed time, and silence.

Morning—Rising bell—leader.

The first session of a leader's camp would be for orientation and the last session given to evaluation. How do we measure spiritual renewal? How do we measure the success of a national leader's camp? That was not easy. Today, as I recall some of the leader's camps, I feel that structure and schedule were not important. The miracles came because people let themselves become vulnerable and open to God. And there were miracles—many of them.

By invitation we also sponsored and I directed leader's camps in Canada, Jamaica, and the West Indies modifying the programs to fit the occasion and the need.

In one camp we had gathered for our closing campfire, when I felt a touch on my arm and in response walked with a well-known pastor slowly through the darkness away from people. Finally we sat on a bench, quiet and silent. Then he began to pray aloud. He confessed to God his infidelity to his wife of many years, thanked God for forgiveness, and pledged a new life of love and honesty. We sat a long time. Finally I prayed, "Thank you, Father, for love—eternal, boundless, believing in us for our best." We sat a few more minutes, clasped hands and left. What a miracle! In a few months he died, and with it the miracle of his freedom from guilt.

One afternoon two of us sat under a tree to share a cup of coffee. My companion was a successful businessman, highly respected, loved by many, generous, and faithful. In a few minutes he wept as he told me how discouraged he was, feeling his life was in vain. Several in his family were in active church service, one a missionary. But he was a failure—he could not do what they had done. We reviewed the story of a boy whose bread and fish were used by God to feed a multitude. I prayed the Lord to help my brother use his bread and fish for God's glory, not to satisfy a desire to excel, just to be God's humble servant. At the campfire that evening I recognized his voice in prayer as he accepted God's plan for his life and renewal came. His closing years were magnificent—a miracle of surrender.

Often we had a leader's camp just prior to the international youth convention. This was true at Camp Caesar, West Virginia, when the convention was in Charleston, West Virginia. Camp Caesar was in a beautiful West Virginia valley. We had about one hundred in attendance. Dean Russell Olt, Earl Martin, Ida Byrd Rowe, Harold Phillips, Adam Miller, Leslie Decker, plus many state and national leaders were in attendance.

You need to know Russell Olt also. He was of German ancestry, tall, pudgy, shaggy eyebrows, dark piercing eyes. As he walked fast he swung his hands at his wrists not elbows. He was socially inept and self-conscious, often covering that with practical jokes. I first got acquainted with him when I was a freshman at Anderson College. On my second Sunday at Anderson University the college sent out teams of students to nearby churches to share about the college, recruit new students, and hopefully get a good offering for the college. The Dean was pastor in Cincinnati, Ohio and a team was sent with him: Elisha Tharpe, Eleanor Irig (later married to Milton Buettner), a couple of others, and I. I stayed with the Dean. We roomed together in the home of a parishioner. The Dean tended to use both sides of the bed. I did not sleep well. The Dean intimidated most of his students, but my experiences that weekend did not leave much room for intimidation. So I took him as he was: gruff exterior, compassionate and tender on the interior, and socially ill at ease—all of it—and we became very close friends to the day of his death years later.

Now, back to Camp Caesar. There was an attractive swimming pool, it was a hot afternoon, and we announced an open swim. One pastor from Oklahoma objected; in Oklahoma the Church of God did not allow mixed swimming. We spent a couple of hours on this topic. Finally Byrum Lee and his wife agreed not to press their opinions. Russell Olt and Ida Byrd were first in the pool. I bless them for courage, leadership, hope, and wisdom. That week we not only talked about mixed bathing but many other related "conscience" questions—going to movies, dating, dancing, flamboyant (or ultra conservative) dressing, make-up (for girls only), tolerance, and generosity for opposing points of view, how to disagree kindly, how to register a minority opinion. We talked openly, sometimes warmly, always freely.

It was quite a week. My brother and his wife were there, as was my wife Gertie. We had some very frank talk about our own family traditions. My mother was conscientious, prayerful, sometimes patient kind, loving, and generous. She also held a rigid theology on all related social questions. All these came to my mind that turbulent week. In her book My Grandfather's Blessings, Dr. Rachel Naomi Reunen tells of a long struggle with fear, going back to her childhood days. Many of her fears were connected with her father. In my faith journey, my fears go back to my mother and her Church of God (Iowa) background.

Finally I was able to surrender to God and peace came. The last night Fred and Doris Shackleton slipped away from the campfire and softly sang "My God and I." I felt elated and hopeful. I felt I was in spiritual renewal. I was lifted into an experience of hope and joy. I left Camp Caesar greatly renewed in Spirit, with more love and hope and peace. I felt good about life and the church. What a way to close the week!

Others shared my feelings, including Bob and Jerry Reardon, Earl Martin, Frances and Bob Clark, Mrs. Rowe, the Dean, and Harold Phillips.

E. Stanley Jones opened the youth convention the next day. In the hotel coffee shop he shared breakfast with a small group of leaders and thanked us for the week of preparation. It was a thinking convention. Dr. E. Stanley Jones was our special speaker for the convention. Everyday at camp we prayed for a special anointing to be upon Dr. Jones. Here's a brief note of explanation. Many of you know of the great passion for missionary witness that laid hold of E. Stanley Jones. It was evident in Charleston. Jones had a delivery that was almost abrupt at times. He did not waste words. On a Saturday morning in Charleston, during breakfast at the convention hotel, a few young people joined him. Like Samuel of old, these were a band of young men whose hearts God had touched. That Saturday it was repeated. Thousands of people have been connected and thousands more spiritually renewed by that "chance" encounter in Charleston! A miracle!

I felt my mother's fears that week. Also I recalled some of the "cultic" fears of the Church of God movement—many just like my mother's. At Camp Caesar when we had fully discussed the swimming issue, Dean Olt and Ida Byrd Rowe were the first two in the pool. Somehow I felt they, and others like them (Earl Martin, E. A. Reardon) would also lead us away from these questions to matters of substance.

I came close to the Lord as I surrendered to him these and other problems.

When the convention was held in Portland, Oregon, we preceded it with a leader's camp in a beautiful setting at a retreat center on the banks of the Columbia River. My memory is filled with names of persons who then were West Coast people who have since become distinguished leaders in their own right. Our convention speaker was Dr. Samuel Moffett, veteran missionary to China. His speaking style was similar to that of Stanley Jones, only more eloquent and dramatic. I recall his story of the Communist drive for control of Shanghai in China. He pictured the defenders inside the wall, supplies and resources dwindling but tenacious and determined. At the same time the massed Communist army was sending wave after wave of soldiers, each wave cut down by the defenders. Moffett said murderous attacks were relentless; finally the guns of the defenders were so hot from heavy firing they were silent and the Communists simply marched in over the bodies of their dead comrades. He called for that level of church consecration, by all of us present. Do you recall the altar response as Moffett said, "What are you willing to give for the cause of Christ?" What living miracles came forward to say, "Here am I, use me." God did. We are still witnessing the results of those commitments.

Each camp was distinctive and different. Santa Rosa, California had been carefully advertised and leaders chosen with care. A planning committee had chosen to explore "The Ministry of the Holy Spirit." All delegates had been invited to prepare by prayer and Bible study. In those days the "orthodox" position was that the first work of grace is forgiveness and salvation. Then there was a "second definite work of grace" in which old nature was pulled out by the roots as one was sanctified by the receiving of the Holy Spirit. As a teenager I had earnestly sought this many times, never to satisfaction. In my early preaching ministry I followed the orthodox line and preached strongly the need for entire sanctification. I did so with some feelings approaching hypocrisy, because I was preaching what I had not fully experienced. Now as we planned for the leader's camp we had determined to openly explore this work of the Holy Spirit.

Santa Rosa was the home of Charles Shultz, the cartoonist of Snoopy, Lucy, and Charlie Brown fame, whom I had come to know personally. That part of California was also home to some of our most conservative congregations. What audacity we had! The physical setting was excellent, right in the middle of redwood trees and productive valleys. The camp began on schedule—everyone in tip-top excitement. Harold Phillips, as one leader, kept a large pair of scissors and to the consternation of some and delight of others, he quickly cut off the bottom half of a necktie—woe to the man who wore an expensive tie, it was ruined. The camp expected only casual dress. In walked the pastor of a large, conservative church, dressed for preaching, and Phillips promptly cut off the necktie. The pastor and wife were angry—very angry! Then for the first large group meeting we began our close look at the ministry of the Holy Spirit—and openly announced our plan to carefully examine our historic doctrine. That did it! Before the session was half finished, this pastor and wife said they were loyal to the Church of God and wanted no part of any heretical departure from our orthodox position and walked out of the camp. What an opening for spiritual renewal!

But it was a great moment of truth and courage. We spent the next several days in a time of refreshing renewal of Holy Spirit leadership. We carefully examined our position, came to a warm appreciation for those who differed from us, and then led to new freedom and true renewal. We talked openly about what God expects of his people in interpersonal relations. We talked of barriers to spiritual renewal—arrogance, closed minds, intolerance, false pride, and so on.

For that part of our journey I thought of this story of another experience with Christy Spaulding Boyer, one of our granddaughters, when she was three or four years old.

We were at the beach by a lake in Michigan. Gwen, Christy, Scott, our three grandchildren, and our daughter Sue and Spencer, her husband, with Gertie and me. Christy had a toy pail and shovel and was digging in the sand. When she had a hole to suit her, she took the pail to the lake and filled it with water, came back to pour it into the hole she had dug. By that time the water had seeped in and the hole was full. Christy said, "Look, Gramps, the lake pushed itself into the hole I dug!" Is that a parable of the ministry of the Holy Spirit? When we clean out the debris and empty our hearts of selfish ambitions, the Holy Spirit moves in. We used to call that "sanctification" and were glad we had it. Now we know better. We know that we are filled with the Holy Spirit for a purpose—for God's purpose. We are to bear fruit, the fruit of the Spirit. Not only will we bear the fruit of the Spirit—love, joy, peace, patience, kindness, goodness, faithfulness, gentleness, and self-control—but we are then in a position to receive the gifts of the Spirit such as are listed in 1 Corinthians 12. Isn't it good to find today more of an emphasis upon the gifts of the Spirit as equipping us for ministry and less upon a mechanical or wooden second work of grace where an experience of entire sanctification became a desired goal.

I have preached many (too many) sermons illustrating how the roots are pulled out and not enough on letting God work in and through us using his gifts for ministry to pull out the tree of evil. The best of it is that: the lake is pushing itself into the hole we have dug in the sand. Didn't Jesus say our heavenly Father is eager to give spiritual gifts to us?

Once we were visiting Sue, Spencer, Gwen, and Christy in their house in Scotland. When bedtime came, Christy went to each of us, gave a kiss, love, and a goodnight hug. When she came to Gertie she said, "I'm sorry, Nana, I just ran out of love, but I'll have some more in the morning!" I thought, here in Santa Rosa, California, that maybe some of us had run out of love, but hoped we would have more in the morning.

Prior to the youth convention in Edmonton, Alberta, Canada, we had a leader's camp also. In Western Canada, there was a strong German constituency, and often the German church and the Canadian church either just went their own ways or lived in almost open hostility. The two did not cooperate or mix well. This was most evident in youth work. German youth were seeking freedom, consolidation within the preservation of original ethnic or national heritage. The leader's camp encouraged this search for higher loyalties and made considerable progress. The youth convention also turned a corner and a new chapter was begun. The convention itself began to transcend national interests. Growth was coming and a fresh renewal of vision and commitment. This was enhanced by the very successful convention later in Toronto—a landmark experience for a few thousand of us. In many ways that became the forerunner of what was to become the World Conference of the Church of God.

X

Smile A While

With much laughter my wife, Gertie, tells an experience she had while on a summer tour as a member of the Anderson College ladies quartet. During their singing a fly entered Gertie's open mouth. As she spluttered, the other ladies stopped singing; the fly came out. As Gertie tells it, the fly shook itself for a moment, then hurried on to a more welcomed spot. Gertie quickly regained her composure, forced herself to show a wide grin, and the women resumed their singing. Sometimes people laugh when the situation really is not funny!

Christian Education Laboratory Schools

Through those early days I had continuing conversations in the forming of state boards of Christian education. This meant conferences with them at least annually. To encourage them we planned some Laboratory Schools in Leadership Education.

The Laboratory School was a one-week experience in intensive demonstration, observation, practice, and evaluation of different methods of teaching using the format of a vacation church school. Trained and experienced master teachers would be the leaders. Members of the state boards of Christian education were the "student teachers" who were the observers. The local church provided children for the various age groups. This would be their vacation church school.

In summary, this is the "LAB" school we planned and I helped as an administrator.

We chose the First Church of God, St. Joseph, Michigan for our school; the pastor was Rev. Glen Marshal, a dear friend for many years. This would be their vacation church school for three summers. Delegates would be members of various state boards of Christian education. Pupils for the class teaching and learning demonstrations would be neighborhood children, their usual vacation church school clientele. There would be classes each morning for beginners (preschool) primary, junior, and junior high. We chose one of our own national staff as director of the school. We would provide all curriculum materials, using a current vacation church school program.

For each age group we selected a master teacher and an associate. Also for each age group a member of our own staff acted as facilitator and secretary. Our laboratory school students were assigned to an age group and all were to be in an orientation session at the beginning (preferably Sunday afternoon.)

A daily schedule was something like this:

7:30 A.M. Morning Devotions and Breakfast (Pastor Marshal was our chaplain and in charge of all devotional activities even though he could assign specific responsibilities to various persons.)

8:15–8:45 Free time—get ready for the day.

9:00–9:30 Preview the plan for the day including observing the teacher in planning.

9:30–11:00 Class sessions with a rest—break.

11:00–11:45 Review and evaluate.

12:00–1:15 Lunch (all meals together in church dining area).

1:15–2:00 Free time.

2:00–3:30 Plan for next session.

3:30–5:00 Evaluate, questions, answers.

5:00–6:00 Free time.

6:00 Dinner.

7:30 Evening vespers.

8:00–8:30 Closing fellowship.

All students (state board members) were silent observers in the morning class sessions, were to be unobtrusive in taking notes, and avoid any noise or unnecessary movement.

All state board members (students) had lodging in private homes of church members. All meals were paid for in the registration fee provided by the women of the church. The outcome of these first "labs" was the hope that state board representatives would establish their own laboratory school at the close of three summers. State boards were urged to send (at state expense) at least two members as student observers. A suggested budget-per-person was provided to each state board.

This experiment validated the laboratory approach to teacher education, but it also showed that we cannot expect volunteer state board members to depend heavily on this particular method of promoting teacher-education.

Smile A While

In all the years that I, as dean, was responsible to arrange for leadership of the Institute at New Orleans, I usually had at least two others to assist in teaching. One year Charles Wilson, one of my colleagues at Warner Press, and I had no other helpers. Charles suggested to me that on Friday afternoon, just before we had our final session, he and I should serve all the delegates ice cream and cake. This would be a surprise to them. We did. While one of us was teaching, the other one purchased the refreshments and arranged them on the long table where the delegates ate their meals. At a given signal I brought the people to the table. We were just ready to say a prayer and eat when someone suggested that each person quote a Bible verse. Let it be said that I am in favor of memorizing and quoting Scripture, but not while the ice cream is melting; however, around the table we went, much to my impatience. When we finally got to the last person, it was a woman with a keen sense of humor. She turned to me and said, "Brother Miller, all I can think of is, 'Rise, Peter, kill and eat.' " "Thank you, Sister. We didn't kill, but we ate and we all laughed!

New Orleans Institute

One day in the 1940s Dr. A. T. Rowe, general manager of Warner Press, called me into his office. It is correct to say that I did not work for him. It is also correct to say that sooner or later almost everyone in the general offices of the Church of God found that almost everybody really did work for Dr. Rowe. That we were not paid for such things does not matter. He was a hardheaded businessman who had been accustomed to telling people, not asking them. Dr. Rowe pulled down a large wall map of the southern United States showing every city where we had an African-American church. As we looked at the map he said his research showed that most of these churches had a pastor who did not get beyond the eighth grade in school.

He had a passionate desire to offer these pastors some help in their ministry. He proposed that the agency leaders in Anderson develop teams of three persons who would offer courses in the practical aspects of pastoral leadership. Warner Press was proposing that it underwrite all financial expenses in such an endeavor. Each team would be responsible for one week of classes. (It later developed that it was not feasible to offer more than a one-week program a year.) The plan called for meetings to be held in the black congregation in New Orleans, where George W. Burns was pastor. Delegates would have lodging and meals provided by the host church, but Warner Press would pay for meals for the delegates at a price to be negotiated. The Company would also provide a free textbook for each delegate. Classes would be held in the daytime and evenings would be a time for inspirational singing, testimonies, and preaching.

When Dr. Rowe had carefully explained all of this to me, he closed by saying that I would be in charge of the entire program. (Who said I didn't work for him?)

It was agreed that the meetings would be in New Orleans in the early spring months. I prayed about this new opportunity for service, talked with my executive committee leaders, and discussed it with other agency leaders. These were the days of strict segregation where we would be serving. My conversations with host pastor Burns indicated that since most of the proposed leaders were white, we should arrange for their lodging and meals to be in downtown hotels.

Before we developed a sort of core curriculum or reached agreement on who would be in the first team of instructors, I began writing for hotel reservations. I sent many letters; all unanswered. Finally I received a warm letter from a clerk at a leading hotel. He was kind and brutally truthful. Our proposed dates coincided with the famed New Orleans Mardi Gras. I had no idea what that was, but I soon learned. The clerks said all hotels in New Orleans and within a hundred miles of the city were fully booked. There was no room either in the Inn—or any other place. I shared all of this with Brother Rowe. In his characteristic way he simply twitched his left shoulder a bit higher than usual for three or four times, and told me to get in touch with our mutual friend, Rev. Charles Cheeks. Charley laughed and assured me we could find some lodging, so I gave the signal for full speed ahead and we started working on the details.

We agreed that for this first meeting the instructors would be Dr. Rowe, using a booklet he had written titled *The Minister and his Ministering*, Dr. Steele C. Smith, and I. Steele had been a pastor in

Oklahoma City for many years and was a good friend. He and I were often associated in leadership roles, though we were so very different. Steele drove his Cadillac and took his ten-year-old son Clarke with him. Many years later Clarke would become a skilled physician in family practice in the Los Angeles area.

A .T. Rowe was about five feet and eight inches in height, white hair always a bit unruly, a raspy but commanding voice, and was always direct and forthright. His left shoulder had a nervous tic and twitched to betray any feelings he had of doubt, anger, unhappiness, or disagreement, I know this full well, for I saw that shoulder twitch many times. He had been a banker in Pittsburgh. He was accustomed to giving not receiving orders—or even occasional suggestions. He had a passion for punctuality. For anyone who gave as an excuse for being late that he was delayed by a long freight train, he simply stated that one should always anticipate such and leave in time to avoid the delay. He had no use for a lazy person, in the ministry or anywhere else. He had strong convictions and I never did see him show fear of anyone or anything. He was always more practical and less emotional than many of his fellow ministers. His voice was loud and clear in preaching or in any meeting and though raspy it was never unkind.

As manager of Gospel Trumpet Company, he had a bitter struggle with labor union organizers. Once he issued an order for all pressroom and bindery employees to meet while he told his reasons for not wanting a union at the Company. When he had finished speaking, he took a piece of chalk and drew a line on the floor, then stated that everyone who agreed with him on this should step across the line; those who did not could look elsewhere for employment, at once most men quickly stepped across the line.

While A. T. (most of us called him A. T. privately, but Dr. Rowe face-to-face) was in the fight with the union organizers, he heard a rumor that there would be some trouble in the plant, perhaps even sabotage. What did A. T. do? He got a gun, climbed to the roof of the building, and on a moonlit night paced in full view with gun in hand. There was no trouble! He demanded absolute loyalty and usually got it. He was impatient with slow and inefficient workers, and usually arranged for them to be terminated. It is noteworthy that when he became chief operating officer, the Company was near bankruptcy.

He marshaled his facts and downsized the labor force, keeping only those who worked hard and well. He also saved the Company from utter ruin financially and left it on solid footing. He was willing to be innovative and daring. He was the one who had this dream of doing some thing practical and fruitful in training leaders of black churches in the southern states.

At New Orleans he showed no hesitation about getting his job done. He took the night train to New Orleans while Steele, Clarke, and I drove. We met Charley Cheeks at the train station on a Monday morning. When A. T. greeted Charles, he said very directly, "Charles, where are we going to find lodging?" The answer was just as direct. "Dr. Rowe," Charles said, "there just ain't no place within a hundred miles." Without blinking an eye, A. T. got all of us in the car and we started driving west out of the city. Many miles later we found some cabins that had vacancy signs. They suited our purpose, so A. T. picked the ones we wanted and paid cash for them for the entire week. On Monday we met our delegates at the local church. A. T. took charge, explained why we were there, what we hoped to accomplish, as well as procedures and rules for the week. A little later, during a recess for lunch, we took him to the railway station and he returned to Anderson. Steele and I went back to the church, got better acquainted with our students, and then talked about the Mardi Gras the next morning. They didn't know much more about this event than I did, but all agreed to have no classes or meetings on this big day— Mardi Gras (Fat Tuesday) the end of long days of revelry and celebration and parades, and the beginning of Lent. We sang and got better acquainted and agreed to meet at eight o'clock Wednesday morning.

Dr. Smith and I scheduled classes for the morning and afternoon Wednesday, Thursday, and Fridays. In the evening we encouraged the delegates to participate, although one of us preached Wednesday and Thursday evening, with delegates participating in lively inspirational singing. We learned many things in this venture.

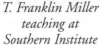

*T. Franklin Miller
teaching at
Southern Institute*

Southern Institute

Throughout the succeeding fifteen years, we held the Institute at a later date to avoid Mardi Gras and early enough not to conflict with farming. Each year I took at least two other leaders, and the three of us alternated our classes. Women of the Church of God, Warner Press, and the Board of Christian Education shared in the expenses. Costs included the books, meals for delegates as furnished by the local church, travel and expenses for the leaders. It was an excellent program and I was glad to serve for many years as the director. Some of the other leaders who participated were: Ida Byrd Rowe, Gene Newberry, Harold Phillips, John W. V. Smith, James Earl Massey, Charles Wilson, Gertie Miller, Howard and Thelma Miller, Kenneth Hall, Clarence and Mildred Hatch, and Hollis Pistole.

To this day there are still former delegates who make the effort to express their appreciation for the Institute. You can measure apples in a basket and water in a jug, but how do you measure the intangibles such as the lasting influence of the New Orleans Institute? We did it for the glory of God and the good of the people, and we already have our reward.

Community Service

I have always enjoyed serving the community and have found involvement in many endeavors. I felt that, since I lived in a community I owed it a little something more than taxes, and have tried to serve where others believed I could: Chamber of Commerce, chair; chair of the Anderson Symphony Orchestra; president of the YMCA; interim director of the YMCA; director of the Anderson Banking Company; board member for Wilson Boys' Club; Salvation Army; Community Hospital; chair of Madison County Comprehensive

President of Rotary

Health Planning Commission, chair; Anderson Rotary Club; two Mayor's Commissions; and other areas of service. Such involvement has brought me many rich friendships in the community; it's been hard work, but a great deal of fun, too!

If community service brought about any worthwhile accomplishments, to God be the glory, for the church has supported me, and God has been good to me. Friends and colleagues believed in me, encouraged, admonished, and patiently taught me, and never stopped praying that I would be faithful. Community service added to my already full schedule and as with other aspects of my ministry, often took me away from home.

Community Affairs—The YMCA

In the early days of the Church of God we were to be "a separate people" and were often considered "queer" and odd because we had little or nothing to do with "man-made organizations," especially if the organization had anything to do with church life. In my Iowa days, some of my classmates at school were members of the local YMCA and enrolled in their popular annual learn to swim campaigns. Since that was off limits to us, I did not attend the YMCA or any of its programs.

This did not make sense to me for many reasons. We lived only a half block from the Cedar River, a treacherous place! Every winter the ice froze to at least sixteen inches. Ice was cut and stored in an ice warehouse to last all summer. But the river had a shifting sand bottom and the ice developed "air pockets." Every winter someone fell through the ice and drowned. The riverbanks were used as dumping places for trash and garbage and were nesting places for rats and muskrats. I was never given any restrictions on either the ice or the riverbanks. I often fished there.

I had a pair of leather high top shoes and clamped on ice skates and a huge sheepskin coat with a large hood. Often in the winter I would walk to the river, put on my skates, and skate far up the river. Then I would turn around, open my coat, throw both arms wide, and let the wind blow me down stream. It was fast. Now I know it was dangerous, high risk, and stupid, but then it was a thrilling sport!

After coming to work in Anderson, I joined the YMCA and one day was elected to membership on the board of directors of the YMCA. It was not long until I was elected chairman of the Anderson YMCA. In the board meetings we had long sessions about its future. I appointed a study committee. As I recall Ned Bardsley, an executive with Delco Remy of General Motors, was named chairman. He had a long association with the YMCA. His committee studied various options such as moving, starting another branch, and remodeling the present facility. The final decision was to do some remodeling of the entire facility and to construct a new swimming pool. This was a major financial involvement, well over $100,000.00. But we had a fund raising campaign, built the new pool, and got most of the other changes made. I gave the dedication prayer for the new pool. I still have not learned to swim, but neither do I think the YMCA is a place of the devil.

Later, when our YMCA executive director resigned, I served with Russell Hulse as interim executive director for most of a year and without pay. I am a director emeritus at the YMCA *and* cannot yet swim!

During some of these years Gertie also was active in the YWCA, serving on the board as vice president. She was invited to serve as president, but none of us could persuade her to accept. She did learn to swim quite well.

Community and The Chamber of Commerce

As a matter of community support, I became a member of Anderson Area Chamber of Commerce while I was with the Board of Christian Education, and continued that while I was at Warner Press.

I was elected to the Chamber's Board of Directors and attended monthly meetings to learn all I could about this organization. Frank Woschitz became executive director. Frank had an interesting career in Anderson. He had served as advisor to the Anderson High School Yearbook. In that capacity he worked closely with Beverley Miller Pitts, daughter of Howard and Thelma Miller; she was keenly interested in journalism. Frank also had a connection with the National Football League Players Association. He edited and published a monthly newsletter for them. Eventually Beverley worked quite closely in this assignment.

Frank was a handsome and charming salesman and helped Beverley have a most

successful high school yearbook. Frank was a tall blond, always with an engaging smile and a strong affirming personality. When he asked me to be chair of the Chamber of Commerce, I was flattered. I felt utterly incompetent for the position. I knew most of the other directors and, for the most part, they were all successful executives in businesses, or doctors, lawyers, and other professionals. While I felt out of place, I knew I could run a meeting as well as any others, so I entered with confidence and determination.

Very early in the year Frank began to promote the annual meeting of the United States Chamber of Commerce in Washington, DC. He hoped to get all of our directors to attend. As it turned out Gertie and I were the only ones who could join Frank and his associate. We went and were glad we did.

The meeting was in Washington, DC. Frank had made our reservations at a hotel used by members of the National Football Players Association, of which he was now a public relations director. When I got in line to register, it was like David vs. Goliath! I stood between two of these big bruisers of the players association. I stretched tall and came just above their belt lines!

Each evening there were rounds of receptions, and Frank took us to a lot of them. They were all alike, so it seemed to me: People to meet, cocktails, hors d'oeuvres, neither Frank's associate, Gertie, nor I touched the cocktails, of course, but Frank did his share and more.

In the daytime we attended serious presentations by the best economists, business leaders, politicians, and government officials.

For me it was very heavy stuff, but I was learning, always learning.

Those were exciting days for business in Anderson. Both divisions of General Motors were expanding and growing. The economy was good. Jack Tidgewell's Anaconda Wire & Cable Company was growing; Emge's Packing was doing well under Pete Elpers; and all three banks were growing and showing profit. Retail sales at the Mall and other stores were good; ALAC was doing a brisk business; Anderson University was growing in every way and making plans for greater growth; Warner Press was having a successful year. Business indicators were good. The Chamber membership drive showed a net gain, and we were solvent.

I was learning something else of tremendous value to me. My horizons were being pushed in every way. My small circle of acquaintances who sincerely loved God and were honest, upright, fair, open-minded, was expanding. Nobody expected me to change my fundamental beliefs. They respected my position in all matters of social, moral, and ethical conduct, and I respected theirs. The narrow and restrictive rigidity which had robbed me of freedom was now giving way to the liberty that is in Christ. I could sing "O Lord, My God ... how great Thou art ..." but also "In Christ there is no east or west in Him no south or north, but one great fellowship of love uniting all mankind." Also I was developing a social conscience with growing space for justice, fairness, equal opportunity before the law and before God, and the essential humanity of the human race.

These experiences were good for me. I have tried, with modest success, to persuade many others to become involved in civic affairs, to find a place of civic service, to give back to the community something beyond what one has received. This can be such a vital a part of the journey, and it surely is our home. Thank you, leaders of business and industry in Madison County, for your patience with me always and for teaching me so much.

XI

Smile A While

Gertie and I were sitting with our grandson, Scott, in a church where both of his parents shared leadership in worship. A bell choir of teenage boys was playing in public for the first time and made several noticeable errors. Scott, a teenager himself, turned to us and said, "Wow, they really are all wadded up." We laughed, but agreed with him.

Warner Press

In the middle of the 1960s Steele C. Smith was president of Warner Press and most of the employees knew he would soon retire as president. There were rumors about who would become his successor. Was it Harold Phillips, Charles Wilson, or Loren Owen? Rumors floated, no one really knew. I didn't nor did I care much. I was happy with my work in Christian education and felt secure in it. I was not prepared for what happened.

One weekend Gertie and I were leading conferences on family living for the church in Pasadena, Texas, where David Cox was pastor. On Saturday morning I began getting long distance phone calls, when I was too busy in my conference to return them. At lunch time I returned a call to Dr. Dale Oldham, chair of the Warner Press Board of Directors. Steele Smith, president, was on the other line. They were calling at the request of the board of directors of Warner Press to see if, after Dr. Smith's retirement, I would accept the nomination as president of the company. I told them I was busy leading conferences and did not have time to worry about that. I finally agreed to meet them for lunch the next Monday. After the weekend activities, Monday came and with it a long discussion about the offer to become president.

I had helped to build Christian education in the Church of God from its very small beginnings. I was well known and had more speaking invitations than I could accept. I had won respect and I had leadership in the field, but I did not know the Warner Press territory. Steele Smith was a successful businessman and had built a strong reputation. Could I take over and build on that? His management style was radically different from mine. Could this transition be made?

We had developed new curriculum materials for the church at Warner Press in which I had a sizable investment of energy. The church needed these new materials. I knew that someone needed to introduce it to the church. We needed a lot of other developments. Steele was surprised that I did not leap at this chance to be a part of such a remarkable history of leadership—D. S. Warner, E. D. Byrum, Charles Brown, Harold Phillips, C. E. Byers, Steele Smith, A. T. Rowe, and Dale Oldham, to name a few persons.

After almost four hours of discussion, I finally told Dale and Steele, "Okay, you may present my name tomorrow. If the vote is negative, okay, I am happy where I am. If the vote is affirmative, I will come and do my best to serve." The board met the next day. In mid afternoon Harold Phillips walked over to my office to say the vote was a strong affirmation. I walked back with Harold to the meeting and received and accepted the formal invitation. For me it was a highly charged hour of emotional energy. I had to return to my office and tell my colleagues and friends what had happened. I told Gertie, Sue, and Tom. We had a sacred family prayer. This was not an easy decision.

The question of salary or benefits had not been raised. It would wait for further discussion. From published reports, of course, I knew that I was the lowest paid of all agency executives. I knew I would not get what Steele was then getting, but that is another story.

The plan was for Steele to stay on as president for one year, and I would work beside or under him as president-elect. During the winter months, Steele would be in Hawaii and I would have full responsibility. In the fall and spring, Steele and I made several trips together attending regional ministers meetings, getting acquainted, and attending receptions in my honor. My greatest sense of disappointment was that Gertie was not with me for these receptions and meetings.

I spent this whole year as president-elect with all the authority and power I needed but I would not use any of it. When Steele was in Hawaii I called him often, asked his judgment on minor matters, and kept him informed as best I could on what was happening.

Meantime several items were on my agenda. For one thing, I was planning my staff. I knew Steele had too many on his staff, but I did not know how I could reduce it easily. Steele did his own hiring. His secretary was Clara Hall, and she kept most personnel files. She interviewed prospective employees, reported to Steele, and then hired them. I needed a personnel director and was about 80 percent decided on Ralph Sprague. I conversed with him and eventually hired him.

Ralph is very thorough and did excellent research on this topic. He knew what was needed, what files to build, what government regulations to study, how to report to me, and how to keep matters confidential. Ralph began the difficult task of creating an employee's manual, and I worked behind the scenes to help. We developed an excellent manual. Before it was printed every aspect of it was carefully reviewed and revised as needed by employees, managers, and our attorney. Ralph also developed his staff, leading them step by step through the manual. His first associate was Anne Mae France. After her husband died she had married Chase Stiers, whose wife had died earlier. Chase was head company carpenter working under Zello Rouse. Ralph also introduced the practice of exit interviews for every person who left the company. He also studied all the literature on government agencies and more than once saved us both failure and embarrassment. Ralph carefully documented every official reprimand and kept us clean on employee relations. He also kept us up to date in wage scales, other benefits, and promotions.

A new government regulation that affected us greatly was the Occupational Safety and Health Administration (OSHA). Compliance is mandatory; failure brought heavy fines. We agreed we must try to comply.

OSHA covers everything imaginable. Our first inspection showed the linoleum tread on one staircase was one inch too narrow, so we replaced it. A larger problem had to do with paper scraps (from our big cutters and trimmers.) For years this had been caught, bundled, and sold. Now OSHA said this created a severe dust hazard, so we had to purchase and use a new incinerator. Zella Rouse, manager, after exhausting appeals, was doing research on equipment. We finally got it installed. On the first day, the first test sent up a huge cloud of black smoke. Some Anderson University pre-law students saw the cloud and without investigation started a legal protest against our act of air pollution. More legal harassment. Some of those students are now (many years later) highly respected Anderson attorneys, and many are my friends. (The journey really is our home.) Anyway the incinerator took care of paper trash.

There was no question on some other staff members—Harold Phillips: Editor-in-Chief; Donald A. Noffsinger: Treasurer; Zello Rouse: Maintenance Director; Robert Shoemaker: Director of Commercial Service Company; Loren Owen: Merchandise Manager; Charles Wilson: Sales Manager; Alan Hart: Manager of Transportation; Clarence Patterson: Printing Manager; and Howard Miller: Manager of Storage and Order Fulfillment.

At the appropriate times, I announced these positions. I arranged to have weekly staff luncheons with staff and encouraged regular reports of promotions or success experiences. We continued to have a weekly employee assembly at 8:00 A.M. with a couple of hymns, scripture, prayer, recognition of birthdays and anniversaries, weddings, special achievements, church events, any new merchandise, and new employees. Somebody figured how much this time cost us in a year, but I felt it was worth it in maintaining employee morale.

For staff meetings, I gave each person a copy of Peter Drucker's book on management. Everyone was supposed to read a chapter and we would talk about it. This was rather heavy stuff for me and for some of them, but it was challenging and good for us all. We also started a publication planning committee made up of editor-in-chief, manager of sales, merchandise manager, finance, and production. This was an effort to help us understand that publishing a book was a total enterprise, and we all had a big stake in it.

At the time I took over, we had a branch operation in San Jose, California, a store in Portland, Oregon, plus the store in Anderson. It was a challenge to develop and keep good managers in all places and to make each one a profitable business.

I tried to keep an open door policy in my office. Any employee could see me just by asking, and we would agree on a time for an appointment. Over a ten-year period I had all kinds of confessions and requests. A man had stolen tools from us. We agreed on an amount of the cost, and he repaid with a small sum every week. A couple was ready for divorce; I got them into Christian counseling. An employee was arrested for murder. I gave challenges to the personnel and some to the managers. One man kept insisting he was underpaid and worth more. We found a "skills test" to which he agreed but did not pass. So it went. I always prayed with the caller, and they respected me.

I worked hard at reminding everyone of our heritage and our mission.

Harold Phillips and I worked together with Kenneth Hall and others to introduce and promote the new curriculum materials. Kenneth Prunty, Mildred Hatch, Kenneth Hall, and I did a lot of traveling for the promotion. There were many workshops to show how to use the material. We worked, as before, very closely with the Board of Christian Education.

It was disturbing that some of our largest churches, though the pastor served on the board, did not use our own material. We did not totally win that fight.

Getting a new hymnal was a huge project. Harold and I named Robert Nicholson general chairperson. The process used is well documented in the hymnal itself and does not need repetition here. It took a lot of money and immeasurable hours of work, but the product shows the standard of excellence toward which the committee worked and, in my judgment, achieved.

Editor Phillips had supported me in the goal of getting back into the publishing of religious books. We arranged a book contest that brought some very good manuscripts plus some quite ordinary. We increased the royalty fee and that helped. We also agreed on a contract with Pyramid Publishers to print paper books—some reprints of our own earlier publications. I recall the success of reprinting C. W. Naylor's, *The Secret of the Singing Heart.*

Bob Shoemaker worked tirelessly to make a success of Commercial Service Company in commercial printing. Some of his notable successes were with "The Guide Light" and the "Delco Remy Clan" both weekly papers by the General Motors Divisions. Their special issues using Indiana artists for seasonal covers were prize winners.

Bill Baxter was star salesman in the wholesale division and greatly loved by all his customers. He had competition, since all of our salesman were loved and trusted by their customers. I cannot name them all, but I will start with Bill, Rodney Whalon, Jim Pletcher, and Harry Dixon.

In our retail store, it was hard to beat Martha Phelps and Sara Lindenmuth, but they also had lots of competition. During camp meeting they put on more clerks and sold a heavy inventory of out of date cards with Bible verses and other obsolete material. "Move it out!" was the motto. My heart (and my feet and back) all hurt for the clerks who worked during camp meeting. I know; I have done it.

Something must be said about free literature. For a long time the World Service Budget had a small amount in it for free literature and it was the president's prerogative to say who got what and when. I was in a church service in another country that was using the new hymnal. All the copies had imprinted the name of a prominent church in the United States, but the name was misspelled. This evidently had been an error in the imprinting and they could not be sold as first class merchandise. They were given without cost to this church. It bothered me that a national church in another country was being given second class treatment to save a few dollars. They can now worship in style and not be ashamed at an imprinted name on their hymnals. I was glad for the privilege of using some of the dedicated free literature money for this venture. As my good friend John Lorton of Florida used to say, "Brother Miller, you belonged to do it that way." Also I found misprinted church bulletins and other materials given as free literature to small or inner city churches. I did not feel it was right to save a few pennies and destroy the dignity of this small church by making them "second class citizens."

We used free literature to help small or newly established churches but we always worked to preserve their dignity. I gave missionaries lots of audio-visual materials, lots of first class material sometimes previously used because of incorrect dating of material.

I used the free literature funds to encourage use of good literature and build goodwill for Warner Press.

Jim Shell was working in the Anderson retail store so he managed the camp meeting tent. He knew that Dr. Kenneth Taylor had just completed *The Living Bible.* Taylor was a professor at Wheaton College. As he commuted daily on the train he started to write the New Testament in language his children would understand and finally completed the New Testament in the *Living Bible.*

Jim arranged for Taylor to be a guest for one day during camp meeting; he came and autographed copies of his book. I took him and Jim and a couple of others to lunch at the Country Club and we discussed ways we could increase sales of the Living Bible.

When I had been president-elect less than a week, I had several managers tell me we must get a computer to stay in business. Some people laughed at the idea and suggested I do the same. I did not. I quietly named a committee to research the matter and named Donald Noffsinger as chair. Weeks later, he and I spent several days in Boston as guests of IBM (International Business Machines). We got the history of computers, along with representatives of several other companies. We did a lot of role playing to demonstrate the value of a computer in our book business. In time we got one, on a lease at first, with option to purchase. It changed forever our way of doing business. The conclusion was obvious: keep up to date with equipment to stay in business.

Alan Hart was a big man—over six feet tall, barrel-chested, and blind in one eye. He was manager of shipping and receiving. He had big ideas. Steele said of Alan, he had "Cadillac tastes on a beer income." He had been elected chairman of the national Truckers and Shippers Association and as such freely treated the members with rich food and wine—at Warner Press expense. I objected but to no avail. Sometimes Alan paid out of his own pocket, more often not. In turn he had been able to get much lower and favorable rates for all our freight shipments—and that was significant. I knew I could not change Alan; he was hand picked by Steele for this job. He held on by sheer bluff and bluster—and by cunning and skill. He was also close to retirement. I decided to make the best of a difficult situation and let Alan stay until retirement.

Meanwhile we were getting ready to build onto the pressroom and order filling area. Alan had a right to submit his requests for loading docks, and he did. He had big ideas.

Gertie and I built our house on a high hill, going north toward a small parking lot of Warner Press. I asked Dr. Smith if that hill would ever be leveled and he said, "No." The very next Spring he had huge bulldozers and trucks and the hill in back of our house was to be moved—as fill in for an old gravel pit south of the office of the Board of Church Extension. Steele spent most of that summer moving that hill a few blocks east and filling in the old gravel pit. When that was done, there was a fine building site for enlarging the pressroom and freight loading. This opened the way for Alan's creative plans. He planned four "wells" for big trucks to brake down into, then by using hydraulic lifts raise or lower the loading docks to truck bed level—a very ambitious program. By selling the plan in advance, Alan Hart got his plan into the works—and we had a truck loading system worthy of the really big freight companies.

There had been talk of getting a new high-speed press, probably five color. Loren Owen wanted it for greeting cards and church bulletins. Bob Shoemaker wanted it for commercial service. I named a study committee and defined the parameters of their study. Clarence Patterson was chair and with him Bob Shoemaker, Loren Owen, and Lloyd Wise and Bill Vetter, two men from the pressroom. They made a thorough study, covering several months. Finally, after gathering information from many other persons, they gave their recommendation that we purchase a Miehle five color press. On their recommendation we entered the order for the press. I recall the day it was delivered, and after it was installed we solemnly dedicated it to the glory of God. Dr. Oldham gave the prayer of dedication.

I have named more than my staff—and others ought to be named: Donald Shields, Jim Tanner, DeLoma Gadberry, James Friend, Dorothy Smith, Phillip Bruzzese, Martha Phelps, Lottie Franklin, Charles Herrington, Leonard Parks, Kenneth Ahrendt, Frank Robeton, Orphah Du Bois, Ruth Leedom, and Anna Mae France. They were capable persons, skilled, gifted, loyal workers, who were also good friends.

For many years there had been discussion of labor unions and, in the A. T. Rowe years, there was considerable organizing activity. He and Steele Smith, his successor, were absolutely opposed to a union in the plant. With my arrival, there was renewed organizing activity. Among the newly hired employees there was a professional union organizer. He lost no time in getting started. We employed the best anti-union lawyer we could get, one with years of successful experience. The employee handbook was surely in our favor, for it listed all benefits plus procedures for handling grievances. Also we had used great care in naming persons to supervising positions. Even so, there were two or three of whom we were suspicious. When we had meetings with supervisors we used great care in all matters, trying hard to be honest, consistent, and fair. In spite of it all, a vote was called for and finally the printer's union won. Don Noffsinger had years of experience in this field, and with his help and the guidance of our attorney, Jack Rogers, we developed an acceptable contract. Those were years filled with a great deal of stress and personality conflict.

We also made a major change in our management staff combining sales and merchandise development into one position, thanks to David Martin, chair of our board of directors. We developed a management disaster plan. In this plan the editor-in-chief shall assume the duties of the president in the event of his inability to serve, until such time as the board of directors could meet and establish an interim leadership team. Other plans were also in place to cover disaster problems.

Another forward step was providing "key man" life insurance to cover financial liability in event a key person was incapacitated. Part-time participation by some key executives made the program more attractive to managers. We did everything we could to provide good leadership for the company, no matter what happened.

At Warner Press, I had many trusted colleagues and allies who helped me in more ways than I can ever tell; they were patient with a newcomer, tactful with suggestions, generous in praise, and cooperative and loyal. I salute them. Many of these became close personal friends.

Many new ventures were to get underway at Warner Press: a new curriculum would be introduced; new books and hymnals were published; new materials were developed; there were new, cooperative ventures with other publishers; there was new equipment; there were building changes. It was a rewarding time, with many exciting adventures unfolding quickly. But, as often happens during times of change, there were some misunderstandings and frustrations. We printed 10,000 Spanish language hymnals and gave them to the Missionary Board. The agreement was that they would distribute the hymnals widely, but request a small fee, and put those amounts back into a revolving fund for other literature. We did the same for Kenya and Tanzania with a Swahili words-only hymnal. I wish I could say the agreement to pay a small fee succeeded; it did not. It was not kept, much to my dismay. Also, most of the recipients did not even know that the hymnals were coming from Warner Press. Doubtless those gifts brought some blessings, anyway.

Dr. Harold Phillips was a very close, trusted colleague, as were other trusted employees. I also relied heavily on counsel from Dr. Herschel Rice and Dr. David Martin. More than once, I flew to Southern California on a "secret mission" to confer with David and Herschel; they faithfully advised and supported me.

The publishing work of the Church of God made significant advances, mostly because I found qualified persons to enlarge and expand their contributions, while I cheered them on from the sidelines. It was a grand experience at Warner Press, but I knew I was not qualified to lead the company into its greatest ventures; that would be for others to do.

God is calling each of us to a life surrendered to Jesus Christ, aspiring always to become the fulfillment of his hopes and dreams for us. Redemptive and forgiving love enfolds us when we fail to live up to God's plan and hopes for achieving our high potential. That tug and pull of divine love is at the heart and center of evangelism. We proclaim the redemption truth and his love constrains us to a full surrender of love, time, talent, and ambition. This is a calling so great it could easily overwhelm us.

XII

Smile A While

In a sermon Pastor Dale Oldham told of two women who were attending a sacred concert, but were not giving attention to it, chatting to each other about some food preparation. There was an unexpected and sudden quiet in the music and the entire audience heard one of the women say, "Anyway, I fried mine in Crisco."

United Way Campaign

Anderson was slow in coming to the United Way of fund raising. The Red Feather or Community Chest, we called it then. Mayor Tom McMahan and Perry House, general manager of Delco Remy plant of General Motors Corporation, asked for an appointment with me. We agreed on lunch in the Warner Press Director's Room. Tom was loved and well-known. He was president of the Hoyt-Wright Company, a men's clothing store. He also had other financial interests in town. He was always jovial and friendly and one of the ten most highly respected leaders in Anderson. He looked you straight in the eyes, he had a quick smile, and was a genial host. Tom could measure a person quickly and, so far as I knew, he was usually correct. He had to be able to judge a person quickly because of his many business ventures and many political appointments. He usually wrote out his prayers and his speeches in longhand and did not often depart from the script.

Perry House was entirely different. He was a career man in General Motors. He was socially shy but always polite and courteous. He was not a quick mixer socially and always seemed at a loss for easy conversation. Some would say he was "all business" and I guess that was true. He was accustomed to having the facts given to him and could then quickly reach a judgment. I have seen him sit through a two hour board meeting without asking a question or giving an opinion. He was a heavy smoker of cigars and normally had one in his mouth. It was my opinion that people loved Tom McMahan; they respected Perry House.

So here were two of Anderson's top leaders coming to be my guests for lunch at Warner Press. They were asking me to direct the annual fund drive for the United Way. They had done their homework and answered all my questions, fears, and objections. They had approached Ray Humphrey, director of the Wilson Boys Club to be my associate and do a lot of the detailed work. They had suggestions for organization that I liked, so I agreed to accept the assignment.

There were two helpful women who worked in the United Way office. We had considerable history to draw on. Ray, as the director of the Wilson Boys and Girls Club, had some experience with fund raising organizations. With all this help I was sure to get all the logistical matters cared for—printing campaign literature and pledge cards, arranging for noon luncheons, kick off meeting, reporting sessions, agency representation, speakers, motivating talks, and so forth. I personally visited most of the agencies to see the program and to meet the personnel first hand. It was a big job, too big for me. The Lord blessed, I really prayed, and he heard.

Two significant things happened. First, we joined the national United Way Organization and could now use their material and lots of guidance. Our local United Way board of directors began functioning in a more professional way. The second thing was that we formally contracted to hire a full time director, Mack Hixon. He had some good experience. He stayed only a short while, but it was a start. He was followed by Gerard Cerney, but that is another chapter. This was my first experience in such an effort and we raised $662,334 of a goal of $675,000. What a year of learning it was for me. I was so glad in future years to see other Church of God agency leaders stepping forward to carry the load: Robert Reitz, Shirell Fox, Robert Reardon, Donald Noffsinger, Robert Nicholson, and others. This is the way it should be. Church of God leaders do not belong on the fringes or in the corners, but out in front carrying heavy loads. The journey truly is our home.

United Way Board

After I had been United Way campaign manager, I was named to membership on the board of directors and was elected president in 1974. I did not feel qualified for this job, but asked the Lord to help and I agreed to serve. It was a big assignment, and I was new to this role. The citizen committee thought I could do the job. The board is supposed to be representative of the community. It sets policies, determines fund raising goals, and sets procedures for determining allocations to member agencies. Regular meetings are held monthly. There are communications with and reports to both state and national United Way organizations.

Carl Dobos was named the 1974 campaign chairperson. He was an interesting character. He was general manager of Guide Lamp Division of General Motors, highly respected as a successful business leader and man of good judgment, honesty, courage, and fair dealing. He was above average height, strong, at home in the out of doors, a fisherman and hunter. He had a strong voice and a commanding presence. He used bits of profanity and often seemed not to know he was being profane. We made quite a team—he a strong Catholic, man of the world; and I, an ordained minister of a small Protestant group called the Church of God, conservative in the theology and social practice.

In one board meeting we were considering for admission a family practice that advocated birth control. The vote was close and in the next meeting I reopened the discussion to encourage all points of view to be expressed. I was criticized for doing this but did it anyway. We had a free discussion. The outcome was the same but most members felt better at having a free discussion. Throughout the year we had standing committees that developed plans and procedures for final allocations of funds.

Carl, as campaign chairman, several other board members, and I attended the annual meeting of the United Way in Chicago. The centerpiece of the program was a huge dinner meeting with Hollywood entertainment. At our table there were about eight of us from the Madison County board. We were so situated that tables around us were served first before we were. The result was that our dinner was served to us just as the program was beginning.

The program was interesting and motivational, but our table was ready for dessert and there was none at our table. When the program ended I went to my room and soon received a phone call from Carl Dobos. "Come back to the dining room!" he said. When I did I found

Carl in conversation with the head waiter who wanted us to go to our rooms and be served dessert there. "Nothing doing!" said Carl. "We paid for service here in the dining room and here it will be." So we sat and were served amid the noise and clutter of waiters cleaning tables—but we had our dessert! I think we all had a new and warm appreciation for Carl Dobos.

Once he told me the story of his life. He was abandoned as a small child and was tossed from one orphanage to another until, in his early teens, he ran away. He lived in a barn for a while, rode freight trains, slept beneath bridges, stole food—a castaway! He survived, got a job, and finally drifted into an automobile assembly plant, worked his way up to foreman, and eventually got into management. Now he was the presiding chief executive officer at Guide Division of General Motors—quite a story!

Carl set new standards for giving to the United Way. He introduced "Fair Share" giving and raised our largest annual budget of $1,043,458. When he retired from General Motors he bought a home on Maryland's Eastern Shore, Gertie's home area. One winter day he surprised us by coming to the door in hunting attire; he gave Gertie a box of frozen Maryland crab cakes—quite a treat for her. Our community, Gertie, and I owe much to Carl Dobos.

Health Care Planning

When Tom McMahan was mayor of Anderson, he named me chairperson of a Comprehensive Health Planning Committee. It was to be representative of Madison County. Members of this committee included Jack Norris, General Motors AFL/CIO representative for community affairs; the administrator of Mercy Hospital in Elwood, Dr. Lawrence Allen, physician, representing the Madison County Medical Society; Frances Snell; persons from government; and a woman from the state board of health. Robert Quinn was to represent the news media. This was truly representative of the county.

I was like a fish out of water. We were to study and assess medical and health needs of the county and make recommendations for changes.

We began by asking agency people how they went about assessing needs. Dr. Allen was helpful, careful not to betray confidential data, but got us started. There was visible competition between the three hospitals, but we kept probing to discuss known but unmet needs in health care.

In discussing personnel, we listed needs under Ministry, General Physical Health, and Specialized Skills (such as cancer, heart, lungs, prostate, mental health, emotional health needs). This opened some doors (at least a small crack) for sharing. Our committee met once a month. We stayed together a couple of years. Perhaps our biggest achievement was the beginning of trust and sharing. I was amazed at the "turf protection" attitude that prevailed at first. I was amazed, also, at how little I knew about the health care in our community.

We also began to list needs of facilities (ambulance, fire safety, police, hospital equipment, ambulances, and so forth). We began to list priorities both in equipment, facilities, and personnel; we also listed these in yearly increments of priority (immediate, two-year, five-year, and so forth). We fumbled a lot for there was very little coordinated planning already in place and no history to guide us.

A woman representing the state of Indiana met with us. Through her we learned of the development of state and area groups that eventually would do what we were trying to do, only in a better-organized pattern. The committee eventually was thanked by Mayor Tom McMahan and disbanded. I had learned a lot. Also I reaffirmed that "the journey is our home."

Service Clubs

When Dr. Rowe proposed me for membership in the Anderson Rotary Club, all I could think of was "What a high honor!" Today I know better. I know this is an opportunity to serve and that is what the good life is all about—service. I then read about Rotary and its founder, Paul Harris, and began to understand the meaning of service to one's community.

All of us are debtors. Someone else crossed uncharted waters and survived chilling snows. Someone else cut the trees and bridged the rivers. Someone else plotted the land and conceived streets and avenues. Someone else found pure water and a way to bring it to where we live. Someone else harnessed the light and lit up my doorway. Someone else planned for, built, and maintained a sewer system.

Someone else watches the night and stops the thugs so I can sleep. Someone else serves. So will I, and I did.

Someone dreamed of encouraging the decorating of yards and houses at Christmas time, and I was asked to be a judge and said, "Yes." I did it for three years. The Anderson Banking Company needed a Church of God agency person as a director. Ignorant me, I said okay and learned to serve. The Anderson Rotary Club needed someone to help plant and maintain 10,000 trees and distribute them ten months later. I did my part each year for several years.

The Rotary Foundation in our local club needed a promoter; I tried. Rotarians World Wide decided to rid the world of Polio by 2000; ignorant me, I tried. As a concerned Rotarian I appointed a committee and asked them to set a goal for donations. They did—$75,000! I almost fainted! That was impossible. So they changed it to $70,000. Then I discovered our local quota was only $23,000, but we began by learning about Polio—a dreaded but preventable disease. We spent almost a year in education and organizing. I took a Rotarian friend with me to get a pledge from one man. He said, "Ask him for at least $500. I explained our mission. He asked how much, I said $10,000! He quietly replied, "I am an old man in poor health, but I'll give you $5,000 for coming to see me and $5,000 to help immunize some boys and girls!"

I called on another man; his friend told me to ask for $1,000. I asked for $7,500. He said okay. I kept on asking and people kept on giving. Our club raised about $120,000. Service is now my business, and I keep on trying to serve. Jesus said it is the way to find life. I am glad to be called a servant and I will continue to try to serve God, church, community, and worthy causes—not forgetting that someone I never saw served me first.

YMCA

When I was an Anderson College freshman I went to the YMCA as a guest. I was introduced to cushion billiards and was fascinated with it. I went as often as I could. In later years I learned to play handball at the Anderson YMCA with Harold Phillips, Robert Reardon, Ernie Owens, and, on occasion, with Dale Oldham. The YMCA was not the center of sin I was taught it was when as a teenager; I needed it and wanted to learn to swim.

I was elected to its board of directors and became chairperson. We had to make some tough choices about modernizing our facilities. We decided to remodel part of the lobby, buy some adjacent lots and erect a new swimming pool, and remodel the small gymnasium. The cost was tremendous, but we started a fund raising program and raised the money. That was the year I pressed Carl Erskine to be a motivational speaker, and thereby got my name in his book, The View from the Dugout. Anyway we got the job done, and I prayed the dedication prayer.

Later I also prayed the dedicatory prayer for the new outside garden. I also completed writing the history of Anderson's YMCA. When our executive director, Norman Walters, resigned and left, Charles Dickmann as board chairperson asked Russell Hulse, retired personnel executive from Delco Remy, and me to serve as interim executive directors for about six months. We did and got the YMCA back in black ink and away from the brink of bankruptcy. I am now a director emeritus.

Chamber of Commerce Strategies and Planning

After I had served as president of the Chamber of Commerce with a new executive and new directors, Michael Collette of Anderson University, a consultant in business organization, was engaged to lead in strategic planning for the Chamber. He asked me to be the chairman of this task force. Of course this was new to me, but I was becoming accustomed to the role of "novice, beginner, one-who-by-now-should-know-but-does-not." So I took the job.

I list all of this here not because I excelled in the work, but to encourage others to step forward and carry a share of responsibility for community affairs. I salute my colleagues who have done this and suggest that since the organizational headquarters of the Church of God is located in Anderson, Indiana, we have a moral obligation to serve where needed in this community. Some have done this so well— Russell Olt, J. A. Morrison, Robert Reitz, Robert S. Nicholson,

Robert Reardon, Paul Tanner, W. E. Reed, Russell Byrum, A. T. Rowe, E. F. Adcock, Duane Hoak, Everett Hartung, Ida Byrd Rowe, Bessie Byrum, Hyla Klabunde, Helen Shoemaker, Beverley Pitts, William Pitts, James Edwards, and Dale Oldham. I am proud to be associated with these persons.

In this same role, I was named to the committee planning for community capital fund programs. Elmo Funk was the chair. He was outgoing, friendly, courageous, and blunt. For years he was Anderson's number one leading Catholic lay person, always at the front ready to serve. We were to assess needs and make recommendations for capital fund projects (buildings, programs, and schedule). Standing in line were St. John's Hospital, the new Community Hospital, the YMCA, and Anderson College. I spoke eloquently for Anderson College. Then I watched Elmo swing into action. He was superb. He first told me all the good things about the College. Dr. Morrison was one of his best friends. The college needed this money. I had made a good case for it, but perhaps the college would do better by waiting a year— more time to prepare and have a successful campaign. Always be well prepared. Plan for success, never for failure.

Then, without taking a breath, he said St. John's Hospital was ready for a campaign now. They needed my help to succeed. I humbly agreed and made a motion that St. John's Hospital should have the first capital funds drive and next year Anderson College. The motion passed. I worked on that campaign and got a plaque for my efforts. I had learned a lot already.

XIII

A Long Journey

This story takes place while I was with the Board of Christian Education and really starts with two busy churchmen: Adam Miller and Russell Olt. Dr. Miller was the executive secretary of the Missionary Board, and thus was familiar with the foreign travel business—
helping arrange itineraries, answering
inquiries about health needs, helping
people get passports, and so forth.
Dean Olt had similar requests but from
a slightly different perspective. He liked
to travel and almost every year led a
tour group of students, faculty members, and other interested travelers to
Europe. Finally Olt and Miller formed
a partnership, the Anderson Travel

Miller with Dean Olt

Bureau (ATB). In spite of only minimal promotion, it grew.

When we had a youth convention in Miami, for example, the ATB also got into the act by working with Pan American Airways to sponsor brief post convention trips to Havana, Cuba. Tom Smith, our national youth director, was one logical person to promote and direct such a tour, but his wife Clara was expecting a baby, so the time was not good for them. He offered it to me. The airline would give free passage to a leader of at least fifteen persons. We had more than thirty interested persons, so Gertie and I could have a free ticket, all expenses paid. The trip was short, only three or four days, so we said, "Yes." How naïve we were. We soon learned how "simple and easy" it was to be a tour director.

Our guide spoke English with a strong Cuban-Spanish accent, but we got along well. It was an informative, instructive, and brief visit to Cuba, but I learned a great deal about being a tour director.

Some years later in Anderson Dean Olt was dying of cancer. I visited him often and, for the last time, just two hours before I left for the Indianapolis airport on a trip around the world to make arrangements for future world conferences of which I was the director. He was a great man, a true friend, and a loyal and trusted companion.

Dr. Adam Miller had arranged my itinerary for this world tour. I would go first to Germany to make arrangements for the next world conference at Essen, then to Hamburg to try to sell some more pastors on the coming conference and get their pledge of support. When this was accomplished, my ticket still had a few days before I could continue. I was staying with Erich and Adeltraut Gajewski; he was the pastor in Hamburg and a powerful and popular preacher. We learned that the Danish Church of God camp meeting was in progress. I told Erich I would pay expenses if he would go with me. We flew to Copenhagen, did about three and one half hours of sightseeing, went to a luncheon meeting of the Copenhagen Rotary Club, then flew on to the camp meeting in Denmark where missionary James Fair was pastor and camp meeting director. We had about a half-hour before the evening service, and the brethren prevailed on me to preach that evening. What a day it was, but the Lord blessed anyway!

The next day we flew back to Hamburg and I continued on my journey going by way of Vienna, Austria, to Damascus, Syria, then to Cairo, Egypt. It was about 4:30 in the morning when I got to Cairo, so I went to the Airline City Office and got breakfast. From there I called Jean Kilmer, a dear friend and now Church of God missionary in Cairo, Egypt. He and Ruth had advance warning of my coming. It was good to be with them and to explore Cairo and other places in Egypt.

We talked about Jerusalem and the Holy Land. The feud between Israel, Jordan, and Lebanon was hot—the United States Navy had warships in several Mediterranean ports, but we went anyway. Jean, Ruth, and I flew to Jerusalem; a half-hour before we got there a curfew was set for 9:00 P.M., all gasoline was rationed, and armed guards with live ammunition placed at every border crossing. I remember going up a stairway in Jerusalem and being accosted by a soldier with a machine gun on the stair landing—demanding to see my ticket and passport. I survived but I was scared. The air was electric with tension in Jerusalem. All air traffic was stopped. We got a hotel and spent a fearful night of anxiety. On top of that I had digestive problems. The next day Ruth persuaded me to eat some yogurt; that helped with my health problem but not my anxieties.

There were other Americans in the same hotel, some who had short wave radio. As best we could, we kept each other informed by relating the latest happenings in the war. I cannot describe the tension and anxiety. The Kilmers were greatly concerned about their daughter, Ann, who was visiting with missionary friends in Alexandria, Egypt. We went to the American Embassy for a word of safety and reassurance. Jean wondered about getting home to Cairo. At the Embassy there was little concern—simply get on any plane flying to USA or Europe, fly to Athens, Rome, or Hamburg, then fly back to Cairo. Nothing to it. In the meantime, we were in Jerusalem. So I hired a Lebanese guide who agreed to take us sight seeing.

We spent three very interesting days seeing so many places of interest in and around Jerusalem, all of Galilee, part of Judea, and many places of historic biblical significance.

After many hours of waiting, one day we heard that a plane would leave soon for Cairo and Alexandria. I gave our guide some "American Green" and the promise of more if he could get us on that plane. Hard to believe, but he did, and soon we were on our way to Cairo. We spent another day and more seeing the pyramids, the Nile, the tombs of former kings, and the museums. Finally I said good bye to the Kilmers and was on my way again.

We came down for brief stops in Damascus and Teheran, and then flew on to Pakistan. My seat on the plane was next to a college student from Canada. When we got to Pakistan we had coffee together and walked around the city a while, but we had very little in common. I did not encourage further acquaintance. He got off the plane the next day at our next stop and did not return. I saw him in the company of two police officers. I humbly thanked the Lord for keeping me from further association with a man who obviously had trouble with the law.

I got off in New Delhi, India, and met Dr. and Mrs. John Phillip, to whom I had sent a letter of introduction. I knew his brother, Koshy, from Anderson University days when he was in a class I taught. John and his wife were most cordial and hospitable. They spent an entire day showing me around New Delhi. Dr. John was the executive secretary of the University Grant's Commission of all India, which meant he had great influence in determining which universities got government grants and how much they would get. One day he arranged for us to have tea with Dr. Rao, the president of the University of New Delhi. It was a very busy day for him and he was delayed at least an hour, but we had tea and a very interesting hour of discussion of adult education as a responsibility of the academic community, and what he personally was doing about it. It was a rewarding and delightful time. A couple of years later Dr. John was invited to be a visiting professor at Anderson University. Several times during the year Gertie and I had the joy of being with them in our home or in theirs for dinner and fellowship. Within the last couple of years Grace died. I have tried with very little success to keep in touch with Dr. John.

From Delhi I went to visit the Taj Mahal, a magnificent monument to the wife of an Indian leader. I cannot adequately describe it; so I will not try. It is magnificent and beautiful. Some years later, when Gertie and I took a tour group around the world, we visited the Taj Mahal again.

My next stop was Calcutta. My flight was on an Indian airplane, a modified DC3. For most of the flight there was only one other passenger; and he did not speak English. Coffee was served and with it one half a papaya. It was not easy to eat, but I managed and it was delicious.

In Calcutta I met with Sydney Johnson and Robert Clark, both Church of God missionaries in India and both good friends of mine. They had expected Dr. Adam Miller to be with me in order to discuss their work with him. We stayed at the Lee Memorial Mission, a Methodist retreat center. Bob and Sydney took me on tours of Calcutta, including pagan temples, homes of wealthy Indians, the Ghetto, and poverty areas. Early one day we went to the Kali Ghat where every day there were cremations in the public square. We saw a family engage in the cremation of their husband and father. We crowded in to the worship service of the goddess Kali, an ugly image with several arms and legs, on a waist high platform, while people placed their offerings on the platform in front of her.

Two incidents from this time still live in my memory. First, two well-dressed men gave a live goat to a priest who after some ceremony cut off its head with one swift stroke of a large sword, then the bloody carcass was offered to the goddess amid more ceremony. I prayed that somehow my life and ministry could vividly demonstrate that the God Jesus revealed is pleased only with the offering of a pure and dedicated life. My second memory is very different. I stood before the Kali altar as a peasant woman came holding only a blossom from a tree. After some quiet moving of her lips, she placed it on the altar. I stood silently and prayed that somehow she and millions like her might find the love and peace of God that is beyond understanding. In that moment, for the first time I felt I knew what motivates missionaries. I wanted to speak to her of Christ, but I could not speak her language.

Calcutta is a big city with some beautiful parks, but also with dirty streets, all kinds of vehicles in heavy traffic, any number of sacred cows idly moving their way slowly, crowds of people in all kinds of dress or "undress," and small shops on either side of the street selling goods and many kinds of merchandise. Bob Clark bought and ate some barbecued meat. I did not. We said goodbye to Bob Clark and he returned to his place of missionary service.

In Calcutta, Sydney Johnson and I met with a son of A. D. Kahn and some other friends at their small church, had worship, and I preached. This was the rainy season and water was deep in the streets. Although Sydney resisted the idea of using a human being as an "animal," we did use a rickshaw twice when the water was almost a foot deep. Sidney and I went on to his place of work, Cuttack. He called it the largest village in India. The house where Sydney and his wife, Jean, lived was the center of what used to be called the "mission compound." It was a large comfortable two-story house. They also had a maidservant. While we were at table eating, she got on hands and knees and washed my feet, a most humbling experience! (We did not wear shoes in the house.)

Jean used her best linen and china and I felt royally entertained. The next day they had a reception for me in their front yard. As guests they had the mayor, other missionaries, and civic leaders. I was not prepared when Sydney introduced me and asked me to bring greetings and a short talk. It was hot with very little shade. I did not have a freshly laundered shirt and wore my dark suit with a coat. All the other men wore the tropical white shirt (tail out) with no necktie. They were comfortable, and I was miserable.

All my life I had heard about the Shelter (a home for girls) and here it was. I visited and got acquainted with the leaders and teachers. It was a moving experience for me. That evening I preached in the church, another humbling experience. Also I had the honor of dedicating the Johnson's young son, a first in the Church of God in India. The visit in Cuttack was educational and inspiring for me. I regretted having to leave the Johnsons. They were so gracious.

The next scheduled stop for me was Hong Kong. Clifford Thor, then a member of the national Board of Christian Education, gave me the address and telephone number of his sister who, with her husband, was a missionary in Hong Kong. Our plane came down in Vietnam, then started on to Hong Kong. It was a night flight and I was awakened by a change in the sound of the engines, and saw a long "tail" of fire from one engine. I called it to the attention of the flight attendant, and she calmly assured me there was not a problem, what I was seeing was normal. But I insisted that in all my flying I had never seen this sort of fire. She finally took a look and said, "Oh, my God" and literally ran to the cockpit. Out came the captain to look and at once that engine was shut down. In a matter of a few minutes the captain spoke on the intercom. There had been a change in our plans and we were now going to Okinawa instead of Hong Kong. We made an emergency landing on the island of Okinawa. We were given vouchers to cover the cost of meals and a hotel room and told we would be here for at least twenty-four hours for engine repair.

In the hotel lobby I found an old copy of "This Week in Okinawa," with a small listing of services at a Nazarene Church. I remembered that Carl Williams, my associate on the Board of Christian Education, had a brother-in-law, Bill Caylor, who had been in Okinawa. On an impulse the next morning, I called the Nazarene pastor. He knew Bill as a next door neighbor and called him to the phone. I identified my dilemma and myself; he came to the hotel and got my suitcase and me. I spent a delightful several hours with the Caylors in a sort of family picnic. I visited the place where they were having a Church of God Sunday school and morning preaching service (without a preacher). I got back to the hotel in time to board my continuing flight to Hong Kong, without further interruption.

After I got into my hotel, the next day I phoned Clifford Thor's sister and identified myself. She and her husband were most gracious and took me to a restaurant for an authentic Chinese dinner. They also helped me with arrangements for some sightseeing the following day. I saw a lot of Hong Kong including a trip to the New Territories on the border with China. I also visited some of the Protestant efforts at church planting. I did not get to meet Dr. Peter and Lavinia Jenkins, later to be in charge of a Church of God hospital and church. I met them in a later trip and they were guests in our home for their farewell dinner in the United States. I also did not meet Mr. Isaac Doone, an astute business man, whose father had been pastor of the Church of God in Shanghai, and a strong ally of Protestant missions in Hong Kong and China. Mr. Doone later became a close friend and guest in our home.

My stay in Hong Kong was limited because of my airline ticket and the time out for repairs in Okinawa. Nonetheless I did some shopping. For Sue I bought a handsome lacquered "hope chest." For Gertie, two end tables, four small carved tables, and wall plaques and had them shipped to me in Anderson in time for Christmas gifts in December. Short as our visit was, I really enjoyed it and was glad to get back on my itinerary, this time to Manila in the Philippine Islands.

The flight to Manila was without accident or incident. At Manila Mr. Carl Kreutz greeted me. Carl had grown up in Iowa, was a friend of Dr. Elver Adcock, went to Anderson College, and he and his wife Hazel were missionaries in China. When the actions of the Revolution were so menacing, Carl and Hazel went to the Philippines to live in Manila. He was employed by the Singer Sewing Machine Company and became an executive in their organization with responsibility for the Philippines. Obviously he was now a very successful businessman. He and Hazel lived in a large and comfortable house with considerable yard space (kept by servants). Carl told me that there was to be the annual meeting dinner of the American Chamber of Commerce that evening and he was planning to take me as his guest. I needed a clean shirt, so he arranged for one of his servants to wash and iron my white shirt and brush and press my well-traveled suit. All of which I gladly accepted and we went to the dinner, a gala affair.

The Kreutz yard had twenty-five or thirty banana trees, and Carl took great pride in showing them to me. I do not know how many varieties he had but there were many. Carl would pull a banana, describe it to me, and by the time I had taken one bite, he had a different one for me. Later we drove through the countryside, and at every crossroad there was someone selling fruit—mostly bananas. Carl would buy a hand of bananas, pull off one for me, and toss the others in a bag. There were also many other tropical fruits and I sampled some, but today was banana day. Strange, but I did not get sick.

Carl took me on a tour of Manila, dodging cars and people. There were scores of Jitney buses (old Jeeps painted in rich colors.) Some had a new chassis and side benches instead of seats. It cost a nickel to ride. I never did learn how far five cents would take one, but I had enough to suit me in just a few minutes. Then Carl and I drove for miles through the country, going all the way up the side of a mountain. We looked across the valley at a beautiful mountain, with a large lake in the middle, and in the middle of the lake was a small mountain, and in the distance another lake with an island in the center. Carl was a most kind host.

During the Japanese invasion of the Philippines, Carl and Hazel had been taken as prisoners of war. They lived in abandoned army barracks, a far, far cry from the palatial home where they had lived. Although it was illegal, Carl kept a diary during the time of his imprisonment by the Japanese and I read large parts of it. They were treated brutally at times. Their food was often water and cold cooked rice. There was a lot of sickness and very little, if any, medical treatment. Carl had to go on forced marches as punishment. There was no reliable news of progress about the American forces liberating the Philippines. Hundreds of prisoners died. Hazel was so undernourished that her mind was affected. Carl and Hazel treated me royally.

Finally it was time to continue my journey and I began the flight to Tokyo, Japan. It was a long flight, but we came down in Guam and Wake Island. I was on a Japan Airline plane and the service was excellent. At the airport there were several to welcome visitors but they were not all there to welcome me. Adam Miller arrived in Tokyo a few days before me and he and I roomed together at Art and Norma Eikamp's home; they were our hosts while in Japan. Most Japanese houses would have a tatami room, a sort of parlor. The floor covering is a soft woven mat, a few inches thick, called a tatami. Adam and I slept on the tatami floor. Our missionaries had a little reception for us. Since it was August 8, our wedding anniversary, I called my dear wife and sent tearful greetings. The missionaries sent to Gertie (and for me) a pair of Japanese teacups with appropriate greetings inscribed.

I led several general confer-ences for the Church of God pastors and Sunday school workers, and some just for the teachers. I used an interpreter, of course, and enjoyed the entire presentation. Phil and Phyllis Kinley, Ann and Nathan Smith, and Arthur and Norma Eikamp were especially helpful to me. I am not sure I helped anyone there, but I really tried; I guess we leave the results with the Lord.

*T. Franklin Miller
Teaching in Japan, World Tour*

As the executive of the National Board of Christian Education, I was eligible for membership in the World Sunday School Association, which I accepted with the con-sent of my board of directors. Plans were being made for a big

*World Tour in Japan with Missionaries
and Church Leaders*

convention in Tokyo and I was registered for that. The world project was called "Religious Pictures for Children Everywhere." Local Sunday schools were encouraged to raise funds to pay for posters. In the Church of God we had several hundred Sunday schools who participated and sent us their offerings. I went to Tokyo carrying a certified check for several hundred dollars for the project.

Several Church of God people registered for the convention; missionaries Nathan and Ann Smith, Arthur and Norma Eikamp, and Phil and Phyllis Kinley, Ernest and Lenora Walters from Flint, Michigan, Adam Miller and I. Helen Weeks, the president of Michigan women of the Church of God, representing the national society, was also there. She carried a large check to pay for an automobile for the Eikamps. They refused the offer. None of their parishioners had an automobile and this could create relational problems. Also if they had a car there would soon be many calls for the missionary to furnish transportation for all sorts of worthy causes. No. Thank you! They did not need or want a car. Helen then suggested a refrigerator and met the same polite but firm refusal. None of her suggestions were acceptable, and she finally gave the money to the Tokyo Tamagawa Girls High School of the Church of God.

The World Sunday School Association convention was a success by any measurements. In corporate worship experience each day we said the Lord's Prayer in unison, each in our own native language. There were more than 25,000 registered delegates coming from ninety-two countries. All were encouraged to wear national costumes and many did. There was plenty of colorful pageantry. By the third session we fell into the stately cadences of the Lord's Prayer, a truly moving experience in worship. On the closing evening, Marian Anderson, a gifted and popular African-American singer, who recently had been refused permission to sing at Constitution Hall in Washington, DC, led a huge choir of more that 250 persons, in singing a part of Handel's Messiah. I was profoundly touched.

There were scores of smaller group sessions, exploring problems and opportunities for Sunday school work around the world, plus countless informal group meetings for fellowship and sharing. It was an emotional mountain top for six days.

Just before the convention, after Adam Miller and Helen Weeks had arrived, Adam, Helen, and I decided to take Arthur and Norma as our guests to a good restaurant. It was a fine place. The problem was that in true Japanese style we sat on cushions or low pillows on the floor, and Helen just could not manage that.

Of course we rode trains and busses for all of our visits and to the convention, and that still called for a lot of walking. I met many other delegates whom I knew and with whom I had worked in the old International Council of Religious Education and some other ecumenical experiences.

The fellowship with so many church workers from all over the world was indescribably rich and inspiring. It was exhilarating to mingle with so many people from so many places and talk about our common concerns, promoting the teaching ministries and Sunday schools. I cherish the experiences of corporate worship, singing the great hymns of the church, the reading of scripture, joining hands as we prayed the Lord's Prayer, the colorful costumes of people of many colors and creeds, the stirring messages, the anthems, the illumination of minds in small conferences, the very presence of God in hotels and trains and meeting rooms. It was a humbling and thrilling experience. This is one event I hope I always remember.

XIV

A couple of days following the convention, Dr. Miller and I left Tokyo on a Japanese Airline plane, deluxe service at coach rates. I enjoyed that flight (many I just endured). It was comfortable and the attendants courteous, kind, and helpful. We came down a couple of times, once for a long refueling on Wake Island, and finally to Honolulu. What a welcome sight.

Dr. Miller had registered us at a good hotel, and we had a very sound sleep, awakening in the morning to the sound of ocean waves lapping the beach. We had a first rate American breakfast, the first for me in a long time. We had a small congregation in Honolulu now being led by an old friend, Proctor Barber, long time pastor in Florida. His wife, Virginia, was a long time friend of my good friends Dr. Anna Smith and Arah Phillips of Texas. Adam and I made contact with Pastor Barber but we were eager to get on with our travel and did not attend their church services. Adam went to Indianapolis and I to Chicago and Philadelphia, where I was to be the keynote speaker for the International Youth Convention of the Church of God.

I finally got to Chicago, only to find there had been a big change in the flight schedule and I could not get a connecting flight to Philadelphia for many hours. I telephoned my brother, Howard, in Anderson, Indiana, and found he and his wife were soon to leave for Philadelphia by car. I arranged for them instead to meet me at the Indianapolis Airport, which they did, and I drove all night with them to Philadelphia. My family had already driven to Philadelphia and was waiting for me at the hotel. What a happy reunion we had.

I had, of course, already prepared my keynote address, which was based on John 1:5. "The light has been shining in the darkness, and the dark has not been able to put it out."

I outlined our dark, hate-filled world; fear, wars, hunger, despair, and uncertainty, illustrating with thumbnail sketches of ministries in Germany, Scandinavia, Italy, Africa, and Egypt; the "Holy Land" of Jordan, Syria, Lebanon, Israel, the paganism in Africa and Asia; India with its temples for prostitution, its idols, worship of pagan gods. I told them how the light is shining through such persons as Gerhart

Klabunde, Erich Gajewski, Helmut Raschpichler, James and Esther Fair, Jean and Ruth Kilmer, Sydney and Jean Johnson, Dr. John Phillip, Aurelius Kahn, Dr. Ivy Kahn, Arthur and Norma Eikamp, Nathan and Ann Smith, Phillip and Phillys Kinley, and a few North American leaders. Then I called for commitment from young people willing to be God's light in this dark world. The Lord blessed and there was a good response. Three days later, Gertie, Tom, Sue, and I were driving back to Anderson, Indiana.

This world trip was the longest trip (in miles and in hours) I ever made in my life. It was a trip always to remember. I am in debt to Dean Olt and Adam Miller for excellent planning of the itinerary and to missionaries and national leaders for warm hospitality and guidance, especially in matters of local or national culture and customs. I am in unpayable debt to my board of directors and the office staff, who helped share the load in my absence and who had urged me to make this trip. I shall always be in a debt of loving gratitude to those who really made it possible, and also paid such a high price for my absence: to my loving wife, our son and daughter; my brother and his wife, who helped behind the scenes, and to a host of others whose prayers and goodwill were underwriting the whole venture. My family carried extra heavy loads but with no apparent chafing of the shoulders. God bless all of those who shared in whatever good I accomplished and made possible such an event.

Commander on the Journey

Fortunately for all of us we do not walk alone on our journey. How lonesome that would be! Some people do and that is most distressing and wearisome.

Much of our teaching in an earlier day was negative and even egotistical. We held that God had given to "us" certain truths, one of which was Christian unity. In different ways we have made our boast—to the exclusion of others. It was important for me, for example, to have as classmates children whose parents were members of community churches, but I had no fellowship with them on Sunday and very little on any other day. They were good, "clean and decent" kids, but they were not a part of the fellowship of "God's people." There was a line of discrimination that was even more pronounced with adults. We were glad to have a Methodist in our Sunday church services, occasionally, but that person should leave the Methodist church—and publicly—to have any continuing fellowship was to be with us.

With that background, it was a problem for me in those teenage days to accept fully "sectarian" Christians. I got over this slowly but not easily. It was okay to play ball (any kind) with Andy Hyland, but I could not learn to swim with him at the YMCA because the classes were all led by "sectarian" leaders. I could not go to the movies with Andy (that was worldly.) Playing billiards at the local YMCA and playing marbles were also worldly: "You might be tempted to bet on the outcome." So it was. Life was lonely on that dismal journey.

But I found company! In high school Miss Terrell taught Spanish and taught us to pray the Lord's Prayer in Spanish. Dr. Owen taught physics and chemistry; he openly shared with us his sense of wonder at God's creation as revealed in both subjects. He was also on the same journey as I was. He told of praying a prayer of thanksgiving to God for making this wonderful world. Even in high school my own ideas of God and what it meant to be Christian were rapidly changing. We had a city wide student prayer meeting for peace among the peoples recently at war. Our town had a city wide two-week campaign with Gypsy Smith. I was named by my church to serve on the platform as an usher each night. (The other person so named was a relative, and he declined to serve.) I went every night, on time, and served faithfully. I learned some new hymns ("Bread of Heaven") but was astounded that so many classmates sang in the choir—songs I also sang sometimes in my church. There were also new songs that spoke to my needs, and Scripture was read every night. (In our church, the Bible was used primarily to introduce the pastor's sermon.) There was also an altar call and people responded. Their prayer was led every night by the pastor of The Episcopal Church. My world was growing so rapidly. The journey was not so lonesome.

Evidently our high schools were having problems of which I knew nothing, but Mr. Couch did. He was school superintendent and had congratulated me on being valedictory speaker. He gave me a marked copy (Matthew 5: the Sermon on the Mount) of the New Testament and a book dealing with courage to be an outspoken Christian. Where were all these sinful sectarian Baptists, Methodists, and Presbyterians now? I prepared that valedictory address carefully, wrote it, and memorized it. My talk had to do with living and doing right always regardless of the cost. I think I hit the target on the city school problem. Many people congratulated me, some on my courage and some on my honesty. I was growing and learning that God, contrary to my earlier teaching, had many people in many different churches.

When I worked at the telephone office before going to college, I learned there were sincere Christians there also, along with many who were not.

At Anderson College it was persons like Russell Olt, Mrs. Rowe, and Dr. Wesley Bransford, pastor of the First Methodist Church who led me into fellowship beyond the small circle of the Church of God. I grew more as an evangelist. I observed that we had some pastors with wide Christian acquaintance and others even narrower than the rigid teaching I had in my home church.

I became pastor in Everett, Massachusetts. Boston did not enlarge its corporate size much through the years, but forty-five or fifty separate municipalities grew up around it. Everett was one—helping to make greater Boston a metropolitan area.

I was welcomed by the local ministerial association and soon named secretary. I formed some warm friendships with some of those pastors; they never were bothered by the small size of our congregation and proved to be true men of God. I also became a regular attendant at some of the weekly lectures and fellowships in the Boston area minister's association; I was growing. In Everett we had a pulpit exchange every year. I preached in the Assembly of God, First Congregational Church, and the Christian Church. I found warm fellowship with many Christians.

We used the baptistry of the Christian Church and joined their choir with our small group and gave a part of Handel's Messiah in our new but small building. Gertie sang soprano solos, our choir director, Ted Johnson, sang tenor solos with others from the Christian Church. I was growing.

I enrolled as a student at Gordon College of Theology and Missions and finally earned my baccalaureate degree—and also found many more true Christians.

When I was named Secretary of Home Missions of the Church of God I went to the annual meeting of the Home Missions Council of North America. I was named a member of that and also became a member of the executive committee. Mrs. Norman Vincent Peale was president. Dr. Mark Dawber, a staunch Episcopalian, was leader of devotions, and asked me one day to give the prayer of blessing at lunch (600 people) and I was blessed. Oh, how I was growing. The executive committee of the Home Mission Council met twice a year or more, once in New York at a hotel and once somewhere in the Midwest.

In those days our general agencies held at least one membership in an appropriate inter-church agency. Dr. Brown and Harold Phillips were on the Uniform Lessons Committee, which had the most denominations represented. Dr. Phillips and Lottie Franklin were on the Committee in Graded Lessons of the International Council of Religious Education (I.C.R.E.). Harold Phillips and Walter Haldeman were on the I.C.R.E. itself. Then Walter Haldeman resigned and I was named to the I.C.R.E. and the executive committee. Adam Miller and later Lowery Quinn were members of the Foreign Missions Conference of North America. Clarence Hatch was on the United Stewardship Council. Roscoe Snowden was on the Commission of Military Chaplains. Nora Hunter and Hallie Patterson were on the Board of Church Women United. I. K. Dawson represented the Department of Evangelism of the old Federal Council of Churches. Dr. Jesse Bader, beloved preacher and speaker, was the executive director. The colleges had their own associations. Each of these had several committees and I served on some of them.

The Home Missions Council had a committee on work with migrants; I was a member of the ministry in Defense Area Ministry to Appalachia. As a member of the I.C.R.E., I was also on the executive committee which met at least twice a year. I served as chair of the Committee on Church School Administration for a total of six years.

I served two terms (six years) as chair of the Committee on Leadership Education. Once there was a demand for a written statement on Philosophy of Christian Leadership Education. Twice statements had been rejected. Lee Gable, the executive of the committee, asked me to prepare a statement, but to read it as the work of a special committee. I did. It was accepted unanimously. I served two terms on the Executive Committee of the I.C.R.E. Denominational Executive's Committee.

I was on the Planning Committee of the United Church School Evangelistic Advance. All of these took lots of time and energy. In 1950 all of these were merged, along with some thirty or more denominations, to form the National Council of Churches. The Church of God did not join, but we kept our memberships on our respective related committees.

Most of the people I worked with in interdenominational responsibilities were humble but gifted persons, Christian, and good friends. I will name a few: Gerald E. Knoff, Edith Lowery, Ruth Peale, Mildred Magnuson, Lee Gable, Randolph Thornton, Mark Dawber, Reuben Mueller, Roy Swim, Luther Weigle, Jack Ketchum, Mary Alice Jones, William Genné, Roy G. Ross, plus our own leaders, Betty Jo Hutchinson, Harold Phillips, Lottie Franklin, Kenneth Hall, Arlene Hall, Mildred Hatch, Otto Linn, and others.

XV

Smile A While

Another experience at Park Place left me frustrated. Again, Pastor Oldham was leading the worship, and I was the preacher. I think I was trying to say we all are open and become vulnerable to temptation. My tongue refused to cooperate and I could not enunciate that word vulnerable. After I had fumbled with the word three or four times, again Pastor Oldham stood beside me with his arm around my shoulder and said, "That is all right, Brother Miller, we all know what it is like to be visited by trouble." I joined him and the congregation in laughing at my blunder. What else could I do? What would you do?

Centennial and World Conference

The value of the world conference had already been recognized by both missionaries and lay leaders in some fifty or more different countries, and it did not need further defense. I was so glad for the privilege of starting the conference and for managing it for the first few events, but welcomed placing the executive leadership of the convention in the hands of the executive council. Now, however, a new assignment was in the making—planning for the Centennial and World Conference which started well in advance. We had some lively discussions about the centennial—one hundred years of what or of whom? We finally agreed it would be the one-hundredth anniversary of the first issue of *The Gospel Trumpet* when D. S. Warner published it. It was also the time when Warner and a few associates had publicly separated themselves from the Winebrenner Church of God and all other similar organizations, to be in God's work without any denominational labels or loyalties.

The executive council named a centennial planning committee and we began our work at once. Also those responsible for planning the next world conference agreed it should meet in Anderson, Indiana, at the time of and in conjunction with our usual June convention which we used to call camp meeting. Dr. W. E. Reed, chief executive of the executive council, and I were asked to serve as co-leaders of the two events—the Centennial Celebration and the World Conference. He and I gradually defined our mutual and our individual roles. We were also to have the privilege of working with the chairperson of the June "Camp Meeting," Mrs. Laura Withrow.

We learned that John W. V. Smith, historian at the Anderson School of Theology and a well-known scholar, was preparing a comprehensive history of this movement we call the Church of God. We encouraged him, as a member of this committee, to keep us informed of progress. We also made it clear that for its optimum effectiveness the book must be ready for public sale prior to the June 1980 meetings.

Dr. Harold L. Phillips, editor-in-chief of Warner Press, also a distinguished Bible scholar, was encouraged to prepare a special edition of *Vital Christianity* and appropriate consultative material, such as our Sunday church school study materials. Each national agency was asked to prepare printed promotional materials in quantities of thirty thousand for inclusion in packets that would be provided for all delegates.

Dr. Shirrel Fox, public relations director for Anderson University, and I agreed to work with the leaders of the Anderson daily newspaper and with staff persons of radio and television stations to prepare appropriate coverage of these various events, giving careful attention to items of local interest in the centennial celebration as well as program speakers of national repute and interest. We agreed to work closely with Laura Withrow in selecting speakers for the mass meetings in Warner Auditorium.

All of us on the committee agreed it would be wise and helpful to identify twenty to twenty-five national leaders from other countries to guide in making major decisions regarding all events. Later the national Women of the Church of God agreed to provide money for expenses of such a meeting provided at least half the number of delegates

World Conference Planning Meeting
Nairobi, Kenya

would be women. The place of meeting was a Baptist retreat center close to Nairobi, Kenya, in East Africa. That became a most effective and productive group for celebration planning. I requested that a proposed cost estimate and anticipated source of income be prepared at once so I would have a budget with which to work. This was discussed, but much to my disappointment was never implemented. One sad result was a huge deficit with no plans for financial recovery for both events.

Brother Reed proposed that we offer free lodging at Anderson University for all foreign registered delegates. No budget for this was discussed or prepared. Later in conversations with officials at Anderson University, Reed learned that all air conditioned dormitory rooms and most of the other rooms close to elevator access were already reserved by the usual and regular June convention delegates. Not everyone was elated with this turn of events, but we all lived with it.

Since I was a former president of the Anderson Chamber of Commerce, I worked through their office to make appropriate arrangements with restaurants and motels for food service for all delegates, and to give us area maps with such listings, delegates transportation on the city transit system, and other such advance planning. Through national and state publications and by direct mail we gave wide publicity to the June events. I contacted several commercial photographers to get agreements for suitable convention coverage. I obtained written welcome greetings from the Indiana governor, the Anderson mayor, and many local professional and business leaders. I was a member of the board of directors of the Anderson Banking Company; in conversation with its president, Mr. Wilbur Roby, I got him to agree to provide a huge "centennial" birthday cake, which local church women supplemented with one hundred extra cakes.

We were able to get individual name badges, color coded to show nationality and language fluency and other relevant information. Dr. Reed (at a cost unknown to us) leased seven thousand pieces of equipment for use in simultaneous translations in English, Spanish, German, and Japanese. I got agreements and time assignments for interpreters in these languages for all of our mass meetings in Warner Auditorium, and for other interpreters to serve in the many smaller group meetings of the World Conference delegates.

We prepared huge welcome signs and greeters for the arrival area at the Indianapolis Airport and provided free transportation to the convention area in Anderson. Actual delegate and lodging assignments took place in the fellowship rooms of Park Place Church of God. I had given training to a large group of Anderson volunteers, some of whom took care of registration and others served as "runners" to assist delegates in getting to their rooms. We had appointed flag bearers and trained them to lead processions in many of the larger conference mass meeting and for the huge march of delegates from the University commons to the football field for the open air celebration.

Leaders in the Yellow Lake Camp Ground in central Indiana and of the Grand Junction, Michigan Church of God campgrounds were prepared to give interpretive tours to delegates who were interested in the history of the early days of the Church of God.

My co-coordinator, Dr. Reed, identified and brought to the conference a California woman one hundred years of age to officially cut the large birthday cake; she had personally know many of our early leaders. Anderson resident and Warner Press personnel director Ralph Sprague accepted the assignment to purchase, inflate with helium gas, tie with six foot long string, and "store" thirty thousand specialty imprinted colorful balloons, and have them ready for use in the morning of the big day of actual celebration of our birthday party. The prepared balloons were "stored" in the low-ceiling open air area of the University's Fine Arts Center.

On the day of the birthday party, thousands of people assembled near the commons area of Anderson University. Anderson churchman Leonard Blevins, armed with a megaphone and electronic amplification equipment, directed the formation of the procession from the Commons Area to the Fine Arts Center where each delegate was given a balloon, moved to the university football field where a speaker's stand and bleachers were in place. For this part of the celebration, Robert Nicholson of Anderson University, served as the master of ceremonies. He gave a welcome greeting, recognized W. E. Reed and some others, led in singing some of the songs commonly sung one hundred years ago, had prayers in several languages, recognized many international leaders and their constituents, and called for the release of thirty thousand balloons each imprinted with an appropriate message!

This was a momentous, inspiring, and moving occasion. Then we all walked back in procession, led again by trumpeters and flags, to a central spot in the campground, for the cutting of the huge birthday cake. This was indeed a marvelous celebration. I cannot adequately describe the spirit of jubilation, joy, and unity we experienced. Where we could we joined hands and hearts, symbolically uniting people of a hundred nations, many races, and languages, all now feeling and seeking the surging of God's redeeming love in redeemed persons. We all felt thrilled with a new commitment to sense God in unity of purpose and proclamation as we renewed the "miracle" of survival and heard the imperious call of a new century of loving service and witness.

Some Interesting and Influential Persons

Over the years, I have been blessed again and again with opportunities to work with and learn from some of the great leaders of the Church of God. In fact, men and women who are outstanding and faithful Christians, regardless of their roots. Here are only a few and only some of the memories I associate with them.

Samuel Hines

My first meeting with Dr. Samuel Hines was when he was the featured speaker for the West Coast Assembly of the Church of God. I had heard of him, of course, but this was my first time to hear him preach. I was impressed. He was not tall, but had piercing light blue eyes and laughter that engaged his entire body. He wore a small goatee. He was a native of Jamaica and spoke with a delightful accent.

Sam had a unique approach to Bible study. He could go at once to the central teaching of a passage. He knew the background of the scripture. He also knew both Hebrew and Greek. He had splendid illustrations that illuminated the scriptures.

Dr. Sam's preaching centered around the theme of reconciliation. In fact, he had a dream of his church being the Center of

Reconciliation Square, reaching far and wide in its message and influence. That influence lives on. His voice is now silent, but the message of reconciliation lives within its seeds of eternity; it will not die.

Gertie and I were invited to Jamaica to lead a retreat for pastors and speakers. The first day Dr. Hines and Dr. Cleve Grant led us in a discussion of the moral and spiritual values in Jamaica and what an ordinary citizen could do about it. I was greatly impressed. I was impressed also when I preached for Brother Hines at the Spanish Town Church in Jamaica and saw first hand what these people were doing to care for the wounded, bringing healing to the hurting, and building bridges of understanding and goodwill.

I saw this demonstrated more vividly as later I preached for Dr. Hines in Washington, DC and saw what that church was doing to bring social justice and equality before the law while reaching out to minister to the hungry, the homeless, the betrayed, the lost, the victims of drug misuse and alcoholism, the signs of abuse and cruelty, and the nurture of a loving, caring church.

I watched Dr. Hines as he served on national and state boards and as he served all of us as chair of the General Assembly. He had a keen sense of humor, an unfailing sensitivity to what was right, and a fairness not often equaled by persons in that high office.

Nora Hunter

Let me tell you about Nora Hunter and her work with missionaries and women of the Church of God. No one who met Nora Hunter could ever forget her! She was sweet, loving, tender, but possessed a will of steel and an unbending determination. She had a vision of people in great need and demonstrated how ordinary women could be used by God to relieve their distress.

She and Gertie's mother, Minnie Andrew, were close friends for many years.

In the days when the national Woman's Missionary Society of the Church of God was being fashioned, Nora Hunter was its center. I recall that June day during the annual camp meeting, 1932, in Anderson, Indiana, when a couple of hundred women gathered near the entrance to the Gospel Trumpet Company on Fifth Street. With Mrs. Hunter leading, all singing, they marched into what later became Byrum Hall. The National Women's Home and Foreign Missionary Society was born that moment. I followed at a short distance, lingered near the door and listened, then realized this was for women only. Nora was elected president and a good one she was.

In Bible times a farmer cut and harvested grain, but allowed women to follow and "glean" what they could from the grain that fell by the wayside. Nora Hunter and her followers were not seeking huge gifts. They were "the gleaners." They were just bringing in their small and modest contributions. An example is the "Penny a Day" envelope; each member was asked to give just a penny each day. It is now a *substantial* part of their annual budget. Their concern was that the money should go directly to missionaries. They also formed a linen closet and kept it stocked with many personal items of clothing available to missionaries. They paid for subscription to magazines that women would want but missionaries could not afford. What a powerful agency this is with such humble beginnings.

Sister Hunter was married but her husband did not travel with her. When they were living in Grand Junction, Michigan, at the Gospel Trumpet Home, it is my understanding that twins were born to them but died in infancy. Their graves may still be seen in the Grand Junction Cemetery.

Mrs. Hunter was a preacher with a passion for urging ordinary women to find and use their talents for the Lord, and she did it well.

What a dynamic force is the power generated by the prayer calendar and Christ's Birthday Offering! It wasn't always a popular cause. She was criticized by pastors who resented losing funds to the cause that she represented. Never once did I hear of her retaliating, but always acting in love. Several times I was with her when she showed the power of love. She made afghans by crocheting and knitting. She made many of them. Once when we had invited her to our house for an evening meal she brought three afghans—one for Gertie, a smaller one for Sue, and one still smaller for Sue's doll! Priceless items they are.

In a convention or rally, she would bring a beautiful afghan and I would help hold it up for all to see. This was her gift to the pastor and his wife. Then she would ask four of us each to hold a corner of the afghan as she called on the entire congregation to give an offering for missionaries, often specifically named, and she would slyly remind us that the afghan was full of holes, and only "folding money" would not fall through to the floor. Then the afghan was presented to the pastor and his wife along with a generous offering for a missionary.

Once I was in a meeting, sitting next to her, as she clicked away at her knitting. When she needed to have a thread cut, but had no scissors; I brought out a small pen knife, cut the thread, and gave her the knife.

Sister Hunter helped me in other ways. Once when I was about twenty years old, I was preaching in Anthony, Kansas, the last night of a revival meeting and Mary Shepherd was the pastor. Nora Hunter was visiting her. I preached on hell and God's judgment that night—the *last* time I ever did. After the service she and Mary Shepherd gently but firmly helped me, a very young evangelist, to see that telling the matchless story of redeeming love would win far more people to Christ than all of my judgment sermons. I am forever grateful!

Thousands of women, and as many men, all owe an unpayable debt to Nora Hunter for her vision, patience, persistence, and courage. The organization she founded has grown beyond all of her and our expectations to a mighty force for God, reaching into every continent to open doors of self-esteem, witness, and evangelism. Its influence cannot be calculated on machines we have, for the books are kept by the Spirit of God.

Strong leaders have given graciously and generously and with daring and courage. The list includes so many whose names have been engaged in the history of the Church of God—Hallie Patterson, Mildred Howard, Frances Tallen, Mary Baker, Nellie Snowden, Pansy Brown, Amanda Hunt, Kay Shively, Doris Dale, Ocie Perry, Mary Achor, Grace Miller, and a thousand times a thousand other names of faithful stewards of the Gospel.

Nora Hunter devoted servant and courageous pioneer, daring breaker of molds, humble spirit. Bless her memory, a dear saint of God!

Dr. W. E. Monk

One of the most colorful ministers of the Church of God was the late Dr. W. E Monk of Texas. He was tall, barrell-chested, and possessed a deep bass voice. His eyes were dark brown. He always wore a goatee and was always positive and affirming. I knew him first when he came to our Cedar Rapids, Iowa, church as a fund-raiser (probably for Anderson College although he could raise money for everything). He punctuated his sentences with a firm period, never a question mark.

He always warmed his audience by telling us how much he loved us, and how fortunate he felt to be our guest preacher. And he smiled. He had some "flip charts" that he used effectively. He talked in large numbers: Always big—either attendance or dollars or goals—always big, always exciting. After he had talked in terms of thousands of dollars, supported visually by well-charted pages, asking for one hundred dollars a person seemed like "chicken feed."

Monk was married, sometimes traveled in a small trailer, but was usually alone. He was a promoter and had learned well all the "tricks of the trade."

During the annual Anderson Camp Meeting, the Board of Church Extension and Home Missions engaged him to be in charge of the 6:00 P.M. open-air services. This was a popular amateur hour. He used many singers and always seemed to enjoy it more than anyone else. He was always smiling—or beaming. Who of us can easily forget his introducing Sister Cotten to sing, "I'll Fly Away, O Glory!"

National agencies called on Dr. Monk for promotion and fund raising. One year he was called to visit churches to promote World Service. On the last day he drove back to Anderson from Northern Michigan, hand washed his car, ate a steak supper—and was worn out! I know, I was by his side. He called the head Sister at St. John's Hospital, asked for a sunny corner room, and checked himself in for a long weekend of (almost) luxury care. Who of us could or would do the same thing today?!

Dr. Monk, wearing a flamboyant Hawaii sport shirt, goateed, microphone in hand, laughing as his big belly shook like a bowl full of jelly, inspired me to give my energies to Christ and the church. He had been involved in Texas politics and had published a book,

Politics to the Pulpit. I thoroughly enjoyed engaging him in private conversation, always flavored with illustrations from Texas politics and local church stories of interest.

Dean Russell Olt

I often roomed with Russell Olt, dean of Anderson College. He wore heavy tortoise shell glasses. He had a booming voice with a tendency to slur or slide over many phrases. He suffered greatly from social inferiority and thus heavily compensated by a commanding demeanor and frequent practical jokes. Many of his students were overwhelmed and threatened by him. He would walk briskly into the classroom maybe a few minutes late and begin talking before he got to his desk. He was also pastor of a church in Cincinnati, Ohio, the year I was a freshman.

Otto F. Linn

I was also greatly influenced by Dr. Otto F. Linn. I knew him before I ever saw him. I was preaching in western Kansas near the Oklahoma line when I first heard his name. Some years prior he had held several revival meetings in that area and there were many who had been converted and baptized under his ministry. He was well loved by many people. I do not know how many congregations were started under his leadership. He was known as a persuasive evangelist who knew and preached the New Testament.

He was a Scandinavian, tall, blond hair, blue eyes, a ready smile, and a very intelligent man. Brother Linn felt the need for more education, so he entered Phillips University at Enid, Oklahoma. Phillips was a school of the Disciples of Christ. Many years later I would study at a sister school, the School of Religion of Butler University at Indianapolis. After Linn graduated from Phillips, he went on to the University of Chicago and earned a Ph.D. in New Testament studies. When I first met him, he was a guest preacher, in a minister's meeting, and in the pulpit he had only his Greek New Testament. He stood and read, interpreting as he read, using only the Greek text. I still remember his sermon on the Beatitudes. It was a powerful sermon, but Dr. Linn did not seem to have much physical stamina. In Boston and in Baltimore, I had watched him bowl with men from his church. He did not have good physical coordination. When he was bowling and released the ball, both legs went out and he kept his balance only by sheer determination and some good fortune. His feet went sideways down the bowling alley, and he barely kept from falling. He was awkward, but determined. The issue was not a bowling score, but an educational philosophy and the future of academic preparation for ministry.

Anderson College had employed Otto Linn. It had a future where he would teach New Testament Greek.

Dr. Linn had seen an operative program at Phillips University and the seminary in particular. The problem was one of schedule. Linn was proposing for Anderson what he had seen at Phillips. Young preachers would have classes Tuesday, Wednesday, Thursday, and Friday until noon. Then students and pastors could drive Friday afternoon to a preaching appointment and return on Monday. That schedule, however, was not agreeable to Dean Olt. It would be self-defeating, he felt, to students intent on the pastoral ministry.

Linn and Olt separated on the issue of academic schedule. The Dean held his ground and would not compromise his stand on adequate time for a liberal arts foundation for pastoral ministry. Two good men, two good ideas, one lost, one won. Dr. Linn became pastor of the Church of God in Dundalk, Maryland in suburban Baltimore.

Dundalk was a ship building town. When Dr. Linn was there, men worked one of three eight-hour shifts each day. Dr. Linn accommodated the church schedule to the ship building business, and had a mid-week service at midnight Wednesday, a men's Bible class at 5:00 or 6:00 o'clock Sunday morning, and other similar adaptations to serve people when and where they could be available. He had a very successful ministry there. I engaged him to preach for us a week in Greater Boston when I was pastor, and I returned the favor by preaching for him for a week.

In those hours together, he told me of his concern for adequate academic preparation for young ministers, including the Phillips University schedule. He also told me of correspondence with Dr. A. F. Gray, who was president of a new school being started in the northwest. Linn was invited to be a speaker for a youth convention in the northwest, to get acquainted and to consider coming as dean of the new school. We know the result. He was welcomed and agreed to move to the northwest to be dean of what is now Warner Pacific College. Here he made a new name for himself and soon was loved by faculty and students. He became a tower of strength at Warner Pacific, and, to their credit, they honored him by naming the new library in his honor. Congratulations to Warner Pacific College for appropriate recognition of a great educator and Christian teacher. For years he represented the Church of God as a member of the Revised Standard Version of the Bible committee, where he served with great distinction. It is regrettable that Anderson College and the School of Theology did not give appropriate recognition to Dr. Linn.

Axchie Bolitho

It was about this time that I met Miss Axchie Bolitho, an unusual woman who was pastor of the Church of God in the Bronx, New York City. In those days we had many "City Missionary Homes." These were unique places. Each was a sort of grand experience in itself. The leaders of the movement established these missionary homes in strategic urban areas; there were many, such as New York, NY; Chicago, IL; Kansas City, KS; Portland, OR; Los Angeles, CA; Boston, MA. Sometimes an existing building was remodeled, at other times an entirely new structure was erected. People who felt called to city missionary work found food and lodging in the "home." Preaching services were not very different from the usual city mission or rescue mission, with an emphasis on providing cheap lodging and meals while the "missionaries" were doing social rescue work, preaching, or distributing literature. There would be training classes for the volunteers, a sort of school for missions. That is how the Anderson Bible Training School got started.

In New York a missionary home had been erected as a dormitory which included a dining area, laundry room, library, and classrooms. This was located in the Bronx and also housed the local congregation for worship services. Miss Bolitho was pastor of this church. She invited me to preach for her for a week while I was pastor of our church in Everett, MA. That week several Church of God foreign missionaries were home on furlough, including Miss Nellie Laughlin from

Lebanon and Syria. She was about fifty years old and an able preacher in her own right. With her was another woman, a companion in work, but not a preacher. Since I lived in New England, I knew Nellie Laughlin's cousin, Julian Laughlin, of Barnett, Vermont; he was a loyal supporter of all Church of God activities.

Miss Bolitho was the missionary home manager and her mother was the cook. They usually had six to twelve people staying in the home. Many service men and women came to stay overnight or for several days. Missionaries also used it for take-off or landing in furlough assignment.

Later Miss Bolitho moved to Anderson, identified with the Women of the Church of God, and then with Warner Press editorial department. Her dentures did not ever fit well, so when she talked we heard the clicking of the loose dentures. I cherish her memory as a dear friend who helped me beyond measure when, at the request of Harold Phillips, editor-in-chief, I wrote a little book on the life and teaching of Jesus. As a proof reader she found and corrected many errors, and she did this for free. She was a dear friend!

Tom A. Smith

Tom A. Smith had made quite a name for himself as a West Coast youth leader, so we hired him to lead our national youth program. He was a handsome fellow, about as tall as I but broader in the shoulders, a light tan complexion, with a ready wit and keen sense of humor. His conversation tended to be sprinkled with clever puns. He was a good golfer, just above average, and natural leader. It's no wonder that he did so well as a youth leader.

In his years with us he was a popular speaker for youth meetings, especially youth conventions. He was an able speaker and writer. Each month he furnished copy for the youth page of *Planning Creatively*, the monthly magazine of the Board of Christian Education.

He became active in interdenominational work, doing well in his assignments for committees. He also fit like a glove in the office, doing his share of the regular assignments.

There was a growing interest in studies of the dynamics of group work. We asked Tom to attend some conferences in this area of concern. He became a well-informed and capable leader in group work, and I depended heavily upon him. He and I often traveled together and became close friends. He suffered from some hearing loss and in coming years he had more health problems. His death brought a great loss to his family and to thousands of close friends—and especially to us.

Irene Smith Caldwell

Irene Smith Caldwell grew up in Oklahoma and in early life showed she had many qualifications of leadership. She took some college classes at Oberlin College and for her thesis wrote a book titled *Solving Church School Problems.* She became a teacher and evangelist and was employed by the national board to do some fieldwork, concentrating on helping smaller congregations with their Sunday school work. She became engaged to marry Dr. Mack M. Caldwell, a widower professor at Warner Pacific College in Portland, Oregon.

After her marriage she attended the University of California in Los Angeles and earned a Ph.D. in education. She was still an active member of the national board when I came to office. I valued her counsel and guidance.

Irene was a large woman, capable of making forceful presentations, and probably was a threat to some board members. She held to very strong ideas about Christian education in the local church. She became the strongest Christian education leader in the Church of God on the West Coast.

After serving many years at Warner Pacific College, she served on the faculty of the Anderson School of Theology, and then went with her husband to join the faculty of Warner Southern College in Lake Wales, Florida. I visited her shortly before her death from an inoperable brain tumor; I received her benediction of blessing before I left, knowing it would be my last visit with her.

Edith Lindenman

Edith Lindenman grew up near Hays, Kansas, and attended a business college in Wichita, before coming to work in the office of Church of God World Service, where I first met her. She was an able typist and bookkeeper, with a pleasant and outgoing personality. She was a close friend of Bessie Willowby. The position at World Service was a special assignment; when it was finished she returned to live on the farm with her parents in western Kansas.

We needed a person like Edith in the office, so when I was in Nebraska with Jeff Germany for a preaching assignment, I asked Jeff to drive me down to Hays, Kansas, to talk with Edith. We found her on the farm, on her hands and knees scrubbing the kitchen floor. She was open to my invitation to work at the Board of Christian Education, so we agreed on her coming. Edith fit well into our office work, and soon she was doing more than her share of work. She was a good solution to our problem.

Edith gradually assumed leadership on the youth conventions and other similar events. The other secretaries worked well with her. It was not long until we promoted Edith to office manager. She also did bookkeeping for the other agencies of which I was treasurer. She was absolutely honest, fair, dependable, loyal, kind, patient, hard-working. She transcribed all of my dictation.

Edith was a close friend. When our children were small, she was their sitter. She and Gertie were close and trusted friends. In her later years she suffered intensely from diabetes complications. What a great loss to many people when she died.

Harry B. Mitchell

Harry B. Mitchell was pastor of the African-American Church of God in Gary, Indiana, when he was elected to membership on the national Board of Christian Education. He was highly respected by his peers in the Black community. He had a job with a connection to the president of United States Steel Corporation. Brother Mitchell was a large man, quite heavy, with a ready smile, and a good manner. He was always courteous, and I found him to be honest and fair in all his dealings. He was an enthusiastic booster for the national board. He often taught one of the Standard Leadership Curriculum courses.

Sometimes in board meetings he got very sleepy and was playfully awakened and teased by other members. He had strong convictions and expressed them freely. He was humble.

Brother Mitchell received from the board a small travel allowance that he could use at his discretion to promote the work of the board. In actual practice, though, he never made a trip without first explaining to me where he was going and why, and asking for my guidance and suggestions. We worked together very well. I loved him like a brother—for that he was.

Dr. Pansy Brown

Dr. Pansy Brown was a member of one of the congregations of the Church of God in Washington, DC, the Third Street Church of God. The pastor then was Brother Benjamin. She was active in Christian education in the local congregation but also in many groups affiliated with the West Middlesex organization of the Church of God.

When I first met Sister Brown she was one of a dozen or so persons we had brought to Anderson to help plan a strategy for helping

African-American churches in Christian education. She was very knowledgeable of the need and was insightful in proposing possible solutions. Later she was involved in leadership of the In-service Training Institute.

She was a beautiful Christian, humble, gifted, honest, deeply concerned about Christian values, and social problems in the family. She and Gertie became close friends. It was my loss that we did not ever get well acquainted.

Cleopatra Jackson (and her husband Raymond)

Mrs. Cleopatra Jackson had a lot of personal charisma. She was married to Raymond Jackson, the powerful preacher and pastor of Black congregations in Detroit, Michigan. There is an interesting story about some correspondence that her husband had.

George Edes was pastor in Kalamazoo, Michigan, following Rev. Hartman (Marvin's grandfather), a patriarch of the old order. "Dad" Hartman did not believe in having much (if any) machinery to run the business affairs of the church where he was pastor. Near the entrance door to the church sanctuary, he had fastened an offering box to the wall. Members deposited there whatever they felt the Lord wanted and one person (usually Pastor Hartman) paid all the bills from the collected money. What has left over could go to the pastor, who served without a salary. After Hartman died, George Edes was called to be pastor.

George discussed with leaders the question of salary and they suggested he write to a few leading congregations nearby to find what they paid their pastor. Such a letter was sent to Raymond Jackson who quickly responded. This congregation paid him a good salary (he gave the amount), paid his taxes, furnished a good automobile, and a credit card to the church for fuel, paid the parsonage bills, gave a generous travel allowance, a personal entertainment fund, and expenses to the various general state and national meetings. For his wife, they provided a weekly maid service, entertainment allowance, "surprise" new clothes frequently, hair dresser allowance, and telephone bills paid. Rev. Jackson ended his letter with these words, "If your church does less it will never amount to anything." The Kalamazoo people got the message.

Cleopatra Jackson believed in equipping people for their calling. She had two or three training sessions (ten weeks each) every year and required attendance. Once a year she had a big evening celebration dinner and awarded recognition certificates. One year I was asked to be the speaker for this event. I took the train and my son, planning to return by overnight Pullman to Anderson.

The evening was impressive and delightful. At their request, I wore my academic doctor's robe and all the other people—students and faculty—wore academic robes. Finally it was over. Tom who had been quiet the whole time and I were taken to the train station. Pastor Ray Jackson gave me an envelope and a hundred dollar bill I found in it. Our room was ready to occupy, so we went in and got ready for bed. Near midnight our car was added to the train coming from New York on its way to St. Louis. The porter called us in time to get dressed and ready to get off at Anderson about 7:00 in the morning. Gertie was there to meet the train. It was a long train and we were on the last car. The conductor told us not to get off; when the train started he would signal for it to stop soon so our car would be closer to the station instead of two blocks away. The train started and he signaled to stop, but nothing happened! We kept gaining speed. He said he could not now stop the train, so Tom and I rode on to Indianapolis.

To make things worse, I was attending Butler University School of Religion and at 8:00 A.M. I was scheduled to give a report in class. Finally we got to Indianapolis and I called Gertie. Then Tom and I had breakfast and eventually got home. We both missed school that day!

James Earl Massey

Dr. James Earl Massey has made a profound impression on my life. I admire his skill as a Bible scholar, his preaching, and his disciplined life. He has been friend, pastor, mentor, teacher, neighbor, guide, and more.

When he was a pastor in Michigan I had the honor of preaching in his pulpit. We stayed in his home and he and his lovely wife, Gwendolyn, were most gracious and hospitable. I admired and praised him when he was speaker on the Christian Brotherhood Hour. Our paths also crossed at the School of Theology when he was dean.

I also recall his superb contribution to the New Orleans Institute several years before. More recently he was named Minister-at-large by the Park Place Church of God in Anderson, Indiana. He has been the principal guest preacher at all of our major meetings and always has given us deeply challenging messages. He has traveled throughout the world as an able teacher and eloquent preacher, frequently honored. He was greatly honored by being named Dean of the Chapel at Tuskegee Institute.

A few years ago Dr. James and Gwendolyn moved to eastern Alabama. He purchased the school building in which Gwen went to school as a child, had the building moved to their home near Greensboro, Alabama, and remodeled it into a beautiful study and library. Gertie and I did have a standing invitation to visit them in the new location but so far it has not been possible. James and Gwendolyn have left a strong impact on our lives; Gertie and I are deeply grateful.

Some Observations on the Journey

The order in which these observations appear is not important. They were jotted down as they came to my mind; some came in recent days, some years ago. Perhaps something in this chapter will become for someone a defining moment. I hope so. Some of these comments are very personal; some grow out of and relate to a corporate life in the religious movement that is a part of my heritage and that I value highly.

- *"Blind as a bat"* —We have all heard that expression. Mammoth Cave, in Kentucky, had thousands of bats that flew out at night to catch insects. Someone tried an experiment—they caught some bats, covered their eyes with tape, and turned them loose. No accidents happened. Their research showed that a flying bat sends out a high-pitched sound, inaudible to the human ear, that echoes back when it hits anything allowing the bat to avoid the object. It flies by the sound of its own echo. So do we all. See Luke 6:37–38. Life is an echo! What signals we send out will return to us: smiles, frowns, love, hope, peace, hatred, selfishness, self-pity, joy, affirming attitudes, negative ideas. Life gives us what we give life!

- *"Are we there yet?"* —On long trips with our family, when the children were small, how often we heard Tom or Sue ask, "Daddy, are we there yet?" I suppose we all ask God that question many times in our journey. God knows the way and the destination, but he reveals it to us only one step at a time. The Old Testament story of the Israelites in the desert after deliverance from Egypt is helpful today. Their food was provided daily, but they had to go out and get it, but only enough for today. Nobody had a freezer so nobody went to the super market and bought supplies to last "through the holidays" or "through the coming storm." Just enough for today was all they gathered. So God guides us, one step at a time. This puts a heavy tax on one's patience—at least on mine. So just for today we ask for his guidance, his strength, his promises, one step at a time. Read Matthew 6:25–34 and Mark 14:12–22.

- *The Other Cheek*—When Mr. Nasser was president of Egypt, I was in Cairo visiting Dr. Cecil Byrd. On one street corner we saw a crowd of people surrounding a man who was beating his wife. It was an unusual sight. He hit her with his open hand on the right cheek, and faster than I can tell you, before she could turn her head, he hit the other cheek with the back of his open hand—all faster than I could imagine. For the first time I understood the full force of Jesus' words in Matthew 5:39. On our journey we will often have to do as Jesus did—turn the other cheek when someone hits us with his open palm. It is never easy!

- **How a Pearl is Made**—Often a clam in the ocean inadvertently gets a grain of sand with its salt water in its shell, and cannot get rid of it. The oyster is irritated, of course, for it cannot digest a grain of sand. It simply forms a secretion around the grain of sand, which hardens, and as layer on layer is secreted the grain of sand becomes a pearl. That's what a clam does with its irritations—it makes pearls out of them. In ancient Athens, so Acts 16 tells us, Paul was irritated as he saw the city was filled with idols being worshiped. He was irritated enough to do something about it and preached that famous sermon on the "true God." In the journey, what do you do when you are irritated? Could you make a pearl? Robert Raikes did a couple of hundred years ago. He was in England's cities and saw many children in forced labor six days a week but idle on Sunday. He was irritated enough to start "Sabbath Schools" in London and thus beginning our modern Sunday school movement. In the Church of God, Nora Hunter was irritated that missionaries were having to live on reduced income and started the Woman's Missionary Society. In Anderson J. T. Wilson, president of the Gospel Trumpet Company, was irritated when he saw all the workers with time to spare, eager to learn, and he started Anderson College. In our journey, you and I will be irritated; the measure of our Christian commitment is what we do with our irritation.

- *How much are pork chops?* —There is a moving story recounted in Luke 8:36–37. Jesus had gone to a lakeside farming community of the Gerasenes. Most of the farmers raised pigs. One of the men had serious mental, emotional, and spiritual problems. People said he was demon possessed, not by one devil but many. He was dangerous to himself and the whole countryside. An appeal was made to Jesus to cast out the demons; they, in turn, asked permission to be cast into a nearby herd of swine. Jesus granted permission. The man was cured of his dementia, but the demons entered the pigs and ran down the precipice and were drowned. Suppose you were one of those farmers—they begged Jesus to leave their country. The price of pork chops was of greater concern than the health of a neighbor. Jesus left. What would we have done? Would you rather have healthy pigs or a healthy neighbor? Maybe it's worth a little thought. Which do we value most?

- *Dust Storms–Life's Storms*—On the journey of life, all of us will sometimes be in very unpleasant circumstances. We will have trouble, maybe disaster, but we can overcome. We can rise above the circumstances.
Severe dust storms and heavy winds were almost a daily event in western Kansas and Oklahoma in the mid 1930s. I cannot describe the severity of the wind. Farmers were getting very high prices for wheat, and many farmers mortgaged their farms to get money to

buy tractors and other machinery and plowed their pasture to plant wheat. The wind blew across those newly plowed acres and sandstorms resulted. Most houses had a storm cellar with an outside entrance, and people found safety there in a severe storm. One day I saw a storm approaching and watched a little bird in a small tree, singing a lovely song! The storm came—fierce and furious. I stood beside the entrance to the storm cellar until the last minute of safety. Just before I ran in, I watched the bird. The wind was already severe and surely would blow all the feathers off the bird. The wind increased, the bird turned to face the wind, opened its wings, and the storm which had threatened to destroy the bird, lifted high, higher, higher—"it mounted up with wings like the eagle." We can be killed by the cruel circumstances, or use them creatively and redemptively to enable us to soar like the eagle! It is part of the journey!

• *How many friends do you have?*—Each year at Christmas time we review our mailing list. For many years we have sent Christmas greetings to a large list. We normally include a hand written personal note (even though we always receive a large number of cards with only a printed name of the sender). On the journey, friends are important, but it takes time to keep in touch. Is it worth it? Some of us think so! The Apostle Paul thought so. Maybe you will agree when you are in the hospital for an extended stay. How wonderful it is to keep in touch with true friends. Don't just wave in passing; keep in touch. It pays. Be at home on the journey with many friends!

• *Friendships*—When Tom and Sue were small, we encouraged them to bring their friends home to meet us. They did. It was rich and rewarding for us. Now in their journey they have rich and rewarding friendships. We had to learn what those friends liked, their tastes in food and social entertainment. They were different from ours. We were happier parents for getting truly acquainted with others on the journey. Jesus did. He was at home in Bethany with Mary, Martha, Lazarus and at Nazareth with friends. Take time on the journey to chat and get really acquainted. This means taking time for school plays, athletics, church choirs, and dates.

- **Leadership on the Journey**—God leads us gently just one step at a time. Sign posts help us stay on the road; they are in the Bible, our awareness of the past, written in history. There are friends who love and care and pray for our well being. Christ is concerned that we enjoy the journey; he has gone the way before us and seeks to guide us. There are dependable mentors—pastors, teachers in school and church schools, often parents and other family members.

   We cannot see the end—the goal—but we trust God knows the way. God never asks us to do something unless he provides the energy and all else needed to get it done. We are not promised good weather or pleasant scenery, but we are never alone; Christ is always with us. We are surrounded by a host of caring others—family and many friends, Christians no longer living who haunt us with their memories of faith and courage. If we make mistakes in our journey, we have the assurance of his forgiveness and redemptive love. This is a Gospel of the second chance.

- **Others on the Journey**—There are many others on the journey at various stages. Some are in poor health; some are lonely; some are plagued with fear and doubts; some are very anxious. All of these need your prayer support and mine. Let us not fail them. Postage rates are increasing, but there are many on the journey who would be cheered beyond description to get a caring note from you. Send it today!

   You are braver and stronger because others prayed for you. As you consider the vast throngs of people who are on the journey, take time to pray for them—for the weak, the timid, the fearing ones; the ones who today have been discouraged and maybe lonely. Can you visualize Jesus Christ kneeling beside you in intimate prayer as you pray for others? If you could leave a note of only twenty-five or thirty words to someone still on the journey, what would the note say?

- **More Observations on the Journey**—It is gratifying to see that more women are preparing for full time service in ministry in our seminaries and colleges. It is most unfortunate that there are so few positions open to their leadership.

The General Assembly is demonstrating more maturity in its handling of controversy and conflict management. It is hoped that this is also true of state and district assemblies.

On our journey we are not alone. Of the many millions of pilgrims on the road, some are or will become close friends. Let us welcome new companions, share with them, learn from them, and encourage each other.

All of us are at different stages in our journey. We did not all start at the same time or place. We might have gifts that differ greatly. We do not all travel at the same speed. Some have a variety of handicaps. We have vastly different opportunities for growth. We really do need each other.

This is really one world in which we live. It is good to see signs of a developing unity among Christians across all separating lines—race, gender, nationality, and denominational background. On our journey we can encourage more of this interchange and move toward the unity for which our Lord prayed (John 17).

In the days before we had the interstate highway system, the roads in the mountainous areas frequently had signs that said, "Danger, Falling Rocks." I recall once we came upon such an area just after rocks had fallen on the road. Driving on these roads was hazardous. In our life journey there are many places where there is danger from falling rocks. The Apostle Paul was well acquainted with such experiences. He wrote of his enduring "afflictions, hardships, beatings, imprisonment, tumults, labors, watching, and hunger" (2 Cor 6:4–6). He recounts these in greater detail in the same letter (2 Cor 5:16): "... for God is with us to give courage, help, guidance, and the assurance that God is always working redemptively for our good."

In my early years as a minister, I was once privileged to attend a small meeting of about twenty persons to hear the famous Christian minister-evangelist, Dr. E. Stanley Jones, give a speech when he was on furlough after his first missionary trip to India. He said a friend asked him what great things he had done in India; his reply was, "Nothing, but India has done so much for me." In my own journey, I have often asked if I was learning anything from my experience on the way. How tragic it is not to keep learning and growing. My prayer is that I will always be a learner, open to new ideas, new truth, new friends, and new mentors. The Girl Scouts used to sing "Make new friends, but keep the old; one is silver and the other gold." We could sing that and do it.

The late Doctor Samuel G. Hines seemed to center his entire ministry on the words of the Apostle Paul in 2 Corinthians 5:18–20. His was indeed a ministry of reconciliation. This assumes that an estrangement exists between persons or in their alienation from God—or both. Who of us does not need this message? I need it all the time in my own journey. It is only as we are reconciled to God through Christ by confession, repentance, forgiveness, restitution, and new commitment that we find peace and full salvation. The interpersonal reconciliation for some of us becomes a daily discipline. It leads to personal growth and fulfillment. It is a most rewarding aspect of the journey. It helps to answer the prayer of Jesus as recorded in John 17:11— "… that all of us may be one…."

In our journey we meet many temptations, not least of which is the pressure to spend more than we can afford. The appeal is constant and usually attractive. "Buy now and save!" "No interest for a year!" "No payments for eighteen months!" Faithful stewardship of life requires integrity and honesty in the way we earn our income, and the same integrity and Christian discipline in the way we use it.

One of the dangers each of us faces on the journey and a danger that we face corporately as a church is that of losing the sharp distinctiveness that marks a true Christian. Someone has said we are in danger of simply blending into the landscape. The message of Jesus was that we are to be in the world but not of the world. Our standards of living, our goals and ambitions, our relationships, our use of time, money, and energy all have to be regularly examined to be sure they come up to God's expectations of us. Here is a striking illustration: Place a live frog in a pan of hot water and it will at once try to jump out. Place a live frog in a pan of cold water, put it on the stove over low heat, and it will not try to jump out. Gradually increase the heat until the water is hot. The frog is now accustomed to warming water and will stay there until the heat kills it. Thus Jesus said in his prayer, "I do not pray that you will take them out of the world, but that you will keep them from the evil one" (John 17:15). The message is clear, and it is for all of us on the journey.

None of us knows the future, and we know only a little of the past. Sometimes we think we would like to know the future, but it is in God's hands and will be shown to us in God's own time. We may find help from the life-story of Abraham. God said to him, "Leave your country, your people, and your father's household and go to the land I will show you" (Gen 12:1). Abraham did and followed the Lord faithfully. That is trust. Our call is no less; we do not have a map or a timetable to follow. We have the daily guidance of our Lord. It is not always easy, but it is safe and it is right. This is our home—the journey with the Lord.

Although there is an increased interconnectedness of people, isolation and provincialism are not dead in the Church of God. They increase the opposition to inclusiveness and cooperation, and what could be the answer to the prayer of Jesus "that they might all be one."

There are increasing signs that many in the Church of God are becoming affluent—just observe the cars they drive, the houses where they live, and where they spend vacations. There are also signs of growing generosity both in spirit and in support of values and causes that are worthy and enduring. As a movement we have "moved across the tracks," but do we maintain the same zeal and dedication?

When Charles Weber was pastor of Bethany Church of God in Detroit, Michigan, I was serving there as visiting preacher for a week of spiritual renewal. One night Pastor Weber gave opportunity for a few minutes of testimonies to God's goodness. One man stood and said in a loud voice, "I am Lazarus, I was dead, but now I am alive in Christ." I thought that was unusual and spoke to Pastor Weber about it later that evening. Charles smiled and said, "Oh, that man *was* Brother Lazarus. That is his name. He is a member of the Greek Congregation of the Church of God in Detroit. Our members all know him and love him." He went on to say that at his work Mr. Lazarus spoke highly of his church, his pastor, the church choir, his Sunday school class and teacher. They were all the "best," and Lazarus invited his friends to come and see for themselves. One day a fellow workman said, "Lazarus, you are always boasting about your wonderful church. What kind of a church do you attend anyway?" Lazarus smiled and said, "I go to the kind of church that turns out men like me!" Don't we all? The enthusiasm of Lazarus is well founded in

Scripture. It is from the Greek *En-Theos*—God in you! That is what our journey should be all about—demonstrating in our lives that God is in us—*En theos.*

Many of these pages have been written while I was in the hospital or in rehabilitation centers recovering from a series of surgeries and post-operative problems.

Over almost two years of this new lifestyle, I have met scores of new people, some of whom have become good friends. Most of these people have talked freely about their own physical and emotional problems. When people learned that I have been a minister for almost seventy-five years, they usually tell me they cannot understand why God has allowed them to have such pain and suffering. They often add, "I don't know why God would cause me to suffer like this." I usually tried to say, as I say now, I cannot believe that the God Jesus revealed would cause such human suffering. Then I would try to review some of the causes of the pain, including but not limited to such as these: parentage and inherited weakness or defect; the birth process (we have a great grandson whose birth process was traumatic and as a result suffers from cerebral palsy); disease from germs, a virus or lack of hygiene; accidents; decisions one makes; decisions other people make; ignorance; contaminated food, water, or air; natural causes; floods; fires; volcanic eruptions; extreme cold or heat; attacks by animals or persons; the emotional trauma from death or similar losses; fears and phobias; haunting memories of failure and fright; unforgiven sin or guilt; the list has only been started. God does not cause such intense suffering; instead God is working redemptively for our good. Romans 8:28 is one of the most misquoted scriptures in the Bible. I recall hearing a president of the United States misquote this verse. He said, "We know that God always works things out for the best." That is often misquoted. The Bible does not promise that everything will "work out for the best." Here is what it really says, "We know that in everything God works for good with those who love him."

Often by the choices we have made, the best has been forfeited. But God will not be permanently frustrated. God takes the results of human choices (less than the best) and works in those situations redemptively to bring something good (not the best). So in our journey, let us rejoice that in everything God is working for our good.

More than sixty years ago the late Dr. Harry Emerson Fosdick, pastor of Riverside Church in New York and greatly loved preacher on *Sunday's Radio Pulpit*, preached a sermon entitled, "Standing by the best in an evil time." It was a development of the words of Jesus to his disciples at the institution of the Lord's Supper, as recorded in Luke 22:28. "It is you who have stood by me through my trials." It was a powerful message, first as he imagined how the disciples felt as they recalled a time when they had not stood with him, then moving to our own examinations of our record of loyalty, making us consider whether we always stand loyally with Christ. That message has relevance to us as we look at our own records. So, in the journey today, do I always stand with Jesus in his trials, or does my loyalty waver?

One of my favorite scripture verses is Philippians 1:6. The Apostle Paul is writing to the congregation he and Silas had started years before, following Paul's vision of a man in Macedonia pleading for help. Paul is recalling how he and Silas witnessed to a group of women and the church at Phillipi was begun (Acts16). Paul surely recalled, also, how he and Silas had been arrested and placed in jail and the remarkable conversion experience of the jailer. Paul surely had many of these memories in his mind as he wrote to his friends, "I am sure that he who began a good work in you will bring it to completion." That is a statement of magnificent faith! God is not through with you; God is still working for the fulfillment of his dreams for you.

A group of us had spent at least a couple of hours in Florence, Italy, at the marble statue of *David*, created by Michelangelo. Our guide then took us down a side street to a shop where, he said, the famous sculptor Michelangelo had often worked and perhaps where he did the carving of his *David*. We looked in awe and amazement, as we saw and examined discarded pieces of marble the sculptor had worked on but that did not come up to his artistic standards. Here was an arm, there a part of a head, here a hand, there an unfinished bust of a man. Our guide suggested that the cast off pieces of marble might have been a part of the sculptor's unfinished masterpiece. There I called to mind these words of Paul and thought that the Philippians were a part of God's unfinished masterpiece. And so are we! God is not finished with us, but will continue with us, for we are God's unfinished masterpiece! All of us are and that is what our journey is all about. Let us join our friends in ancient Phillippi of Macedonia, and rejoice that God is still working out his divine creative genius in our lives.

France is noted for its special perfumes. In France there is a rural area where roses are grown. Workers gather the rose petals to use in making perfume. It is said that these workers handle so many rose petals that the aroma of the rose remains on their hands, they can always be identified by the rose aroma they carry on their hands. Is it too much to say that in our faith journey we should live so close to our Savior Jesus Christ that there is no error made in our identity? The aroma of Christ becomes part of our very being.

One person confessed, "The song I came to sing will not be sung. I gave all of my energy to tuning and retuning my instrument." Some people die with their music still in them. In our journey let us be prepared to use our energies to the glory of God and for the good of persons; let us sing our song now.

A Final Word

Finally: I thank the Lord for salvation, guidance, healing, comfort, protection, and divine leadership for a lifetime, since I first surrendered my life to him in boyhood days. No adding machine I have can count answers to prayer or times of his presence standing beside me in temptation, severe trouble, illness, and troubled waters. I thank my lovely and loving wife, Gertie; my parents; my brother and sisters; thousands of acquaintances; hundreds of friends, teachers, pastors, fellow executives; our son, Tom and his wife Sandra, their son Scott; our daughter, Sue and her husband, Spencer, and their daughters, Gwen and Christy, and their spouses and families; our friends that include Dale and Dorothy, Beverley and Bill and their families; the warm and redemptive groups who have helped me a thousand times over. To missionaries and national leaders in many other countries, I owe an unpayable debt of hospitality, friendship, guidance, and love. All of our extended family have shown their love and affection many, many times over, and I am most grateful. May all of you find the same divine friendship and redeeming love I have found in Jesus Christ.